Letts GCSE

Success

Revision Guide

Additional
Science
Higher

Brian Arnold • Hannah Kingston • Emma Poole

Contents

Physics

Cells

Cells are the building blocks of life. All living things are made up of cells. A living thing is called an organism. Plants and animals are organisms.

Animal and plant cells

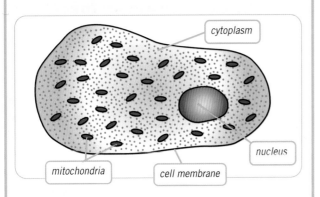

Both animal and plant cells have:
a nucleus
cytoplasm
a cell membrane
mitochondria
ribosomes

Only plant cells have:
a cell wall
a vacuole
chloroplasts

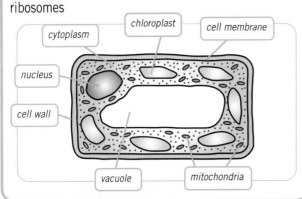

Parts of the cell

- **Nucleus** – The nucleus controls all the chemical processes that take place inside the cell. It also contains **all the information** needed to produce a new living organism.
- **Cytoplasm** – This is where the **chemical reactions** take place. Chemical reactions are controlled by enzymes.
- **Cell membrane** – This controls what passes **in and out** of the cell.
- **Mitochondria** – Where **respiration** takes place. Glucose and oxygen are changed into energy.
- **Ribosomes** – The ribosomes are found in the cytoplasm and are the site of protein synthesis.
- **Cell wall** – This is made of **cellulose**, which gives a plant cell **strength and support**.
- **Vacuole** – This contains a weak solution of salt and sugar called **cell sap**. The vacuole also gives the cell support.
- **Chloroplasts** – These contain a green substance called **chlorophyll**. This absorbs the sun's energy so that the plant can **make its own food**.

💡 *Make sure you know the similarities and, in particular, the differences between an animal and a plant cell.*

Specialised animal cells

Specialised cells can change their shape and differentiate in order to carry out a particular job. It's a bit like a factory where each person has their own job and is more efficient this way.

A sperm cell has a **tail** which enables it to swim towards the egg. Its head is also streamlined to aid swimming.

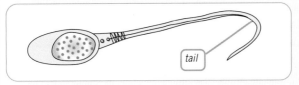

Red blood cells have **no nucleus** so there is more room for oxygen. They are also **biconcave** for maximum surface area.

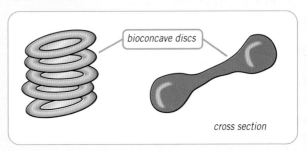

Specialised plant cells

Root hair cells are long and thin to absorb water and minerals from the soil.

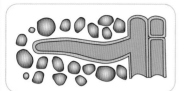

Palisade cells have **lots of chloroplasts**. They are near the surface of the leaf and so can absorb sunlight for photosynthesis.

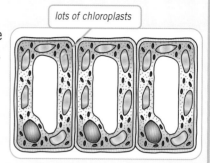

lots of chloroplasts

Multicellular organisms

Multicellular means 'made up of many cells'. Humans are multicellular. Being multicellular means that an organism can be larger and more complex because the organism's cells have differentiated into many different types of cell, like nerve cells and muscle cells.

Unicellular organisms, made up of only one cell, have a large surface area to volume ratio and can rely on simple diffusion to meet their needs. An example of a unicellular animal is the amoeba.

Multicellular organisms require more specialised cells, grouped into tissues and organs, to meet their many life processes such as support, coordination and transport.

Growth

Animal cells grow from a fertilised egg by a process called mitosis: cells copy their genetic information and then divide into identical cells. The cell continues to divide and grow and then differentiates into different types of cells, tissues and organs until it makes a complete organism. Once maximum growth is reached, cells only divide to repair and replace: specialisation does not occur.

Plant cells grow by their cells enlarging: cell division only takes place at the tips of shoots and roots.

Some plant cells behave differently from animal cells. They can continue to grow and differentiate throughout life, whereas animal cells lose this ability when they mature.

This can be demonstrated by taking cuttings from plants. Each of these cuttings, which are simply sections of a plant, is capable of growing into an identical plant under the right conditions.

Human growth

The main phases of human growth are infancy, puberty and maturity.

Humans grow at different rates throughout these stages. For example, in early infancy, growth is concentrated on the trunk and head, with the arms and legs getting longer at the age of six. This is because babies are less mobile during infancy and their growth needs to concentrate on digestion, in the trunk area.

During puberty, there is a growth spurt. Once maturity has been reached, humans actually lose a little height.

Babies in the womb exhibit different growth rates for different parts of their body. At first the head is much larger than the rest of the body but, about half way through pregnancy, the body begins to catch up.

Once born, weight and head size (if plotted on growth curves) can indicate growth problems, if they lie outside the normal range.

QUICK TEST

1. Name three differences between a plant and an animal cell.
2. Name five similarities between a plant and an animal cell.
3. What does the cell membrane do?
4. What does the cell wall do?
5. What occurs in the mitochondria?
6. What is a 'specialised' cell?
7. Which is the only cell not to have a nucleus?

Diffusion and osmosis

Diffusion and *osmosis* are processes that involve the movement of particles through membranes.

Simple diffusion

The definition of diffusion is:

The movement of particles from an area of high concentration to an area of low concentration until they are evenly spread out.

Diffusion occurs in gases or to any substance in a solution.

There are two rules to remember:
- The **larger** the particle, the **slower** the rate of diffusion.
- The greater the difference in concentration, the greater the rate of diffusion. The difference is called a **concentration gradient**.

Example of diffusion in plant cells

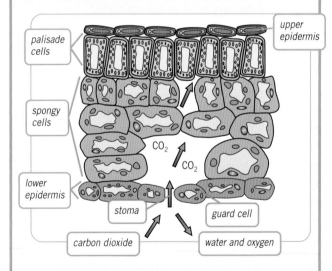

A plant needs carbon dioxide for **photosynthesis**. Carbon dioxide **diffuses into** the leaf via the stomata (holes) found on the underside of a leaf.

A leaf produces oxygen and water vapour. Oxygen and water vapour **diffuse out of** the stomata.

Diffusion of water vapour occurs because there is a lot of it inside the leaf and less of it on the outside. This occurs much quicker in **hot, dry, windy conditions**.

Example of diffusion in animal cells

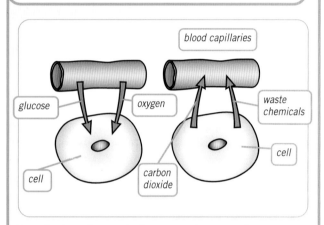

Your body cells need glucose and oxygen for **respiration**. These are both carried in blood. When blood reaches the cells, the oxygen and glucose **diffuse** into the cell.

Your cells produce waste and carbon dioxide. These **diffuse** out of the cells into the blood. The exchange of carbon dioxide and oxygen between the alveoli in the lungs and the blood is also an example of diffusion.

Osmosis – a special case of diffusion 1

Every cell is surrounded by a cell membrane, which has tiny holes in it. This membrane is **partially permeable**. It allows small molecules to pass through, but not larger ones.

The definition of osmosis is:

The movement of water molecules from an area of high water concentration (weak/dilute solution) to an area of low water concentration (strong/concentrated solution) through a partially-permeable membrane.

Water actually moves both ways to try and even up the concentrations. If there is more movement one way, we say there is a **net movement** of water into the area where there is less water.

Osmosis – a special case of diffusion 2

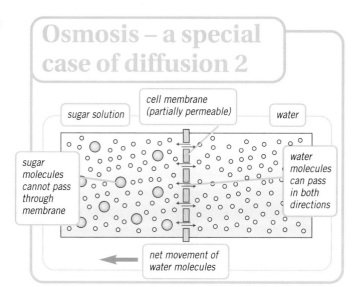

Osmosis in animal cells

Animal cells have no cell wall to stop them swelling. So if they are placed in pure water, they take in water by **osmosis** until they burst!

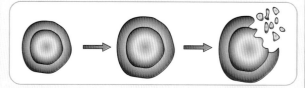

💡 *Make sure that you learn the definitions of diffusion and osmosis.*

Example of osmosis in plant cells

Root hairs take in water from the soil by **osmosis**. Water continues to move along the cells of the root up the xylem to the leaf. All the time water is moving to areas of lower water concentration.

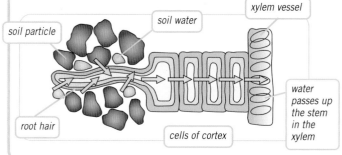

Osmosis makes plant cells swell up. The water moves into the plant cell vacuole and pushes against the cell wall. The cell wall stops the cell from bursting. We say that the cell is **turgid**. This also gives the stem of plants support. If a plant is lacking in water, it wilts and the cells become **flaccid**, as water has moved out of the cells.

If a lot of water leaves the cell then the cytoplasm starts to peel away from the cell wall. We say the cell has undergone **plasmolysis**.

How water travels through a plant

Water is absorbed from the soil by root hairs on the root. The root hairs provide maximum surface area for osmosis. **Xylem tissue** transports water and minerals from the roots to the stem and leaves. **Transpiration** is the movement and eventual loss of water through the plant, in a process sometimes called the transpiration stream. It begins in the roots and ends in the leaves, where it is lost by evaporation through the stomata on the underside of a leaf. **Guard cells** control the **opening and closing of the stomata**.

The stomata may also be closed in very dry conditions in order to reduce transpiration. **Plants that live in hot dry climates have fewer stomata and also a thick, waxy cuticle to reduce evaporation from the leaf's surface.** The transpiration stream provides the plant with water for cooling, photosynthesis, support and the movement of minerals (dissolved in water). Transpiration is fastest when it is **hot, dry and windy**.

QUICK TEST

1. Give an example of diffusion in plant cells.
2. What is a 'partially permeable membrane'?
3. What substance moves by osmosis?
4. What happens to plant cells that take up water by osmosis?
5. What happens to plant cells that lose water by osmosis?
6. Why do animal cells burst when placed in pure water?
7. What does the term 'net movement' mean?
8. Under what conditions is transpiration fastest?

Photosynthesis

Photosynthesis

Photosynthesis is a chemical process that plants use to make their food (**glucose**) and oxygen, using light energy from the sun. It occurs in leaves that contain chlorophyll, a green pigment that absorbs sunlight contained in chloroplasts of some plant cells. Plants also need carbon dioxide and water for photosynthesis. Photosynthesis only takes place in the light.

The word equation of photosynthesis is:

$$\text{carbon dioxide + water} \xrightarrow[\text{chlorophyll}]{\text{light}} \text{glucose + oxygen}$$

The balanced symbol equation is:

$$6CO_2 + 6H_2O \rightarrow C_6H_{12}O_6 + 6O_2$$

Uses of glucose

Some glucose is used in respiration, which plants carry out constantly. Other uses include converting the rest of the glucose into useful substances, such as:

- **insoluble starch** stored in the roots, particularly in the winter
- **cellulose**, which is needed for cell walls

- **glucose**, which can also be combined with other substances, such as nitrates obtained from the soil, and turned into **proteins**
- **lipids and oils**, which are also formed from glucose and stored in the seeds of the plant.

Use of plants

Plants are extremely important to animals and humans, not least as a food source. They have many more, different uses.

Plants supply animals with oxygen when they photosynthesise, and we supply them with carbon dioxide to photosynthesise. Plants use some of the oxygen they produce to carry out respiration. Respiration provides them with energy to grow and increase their biomass (living mass). We can then use this biomass for food, for us and for livestock; or use it as a fuel, as in the case of wood. Sugar cane can be

fermented into alcohol that is used as a fuel in Brazil (called biofuel). Plants can also be used to make fibres, such as cotton, and employed for pharmaceutical purposes (medicines).

Farmers and horticulturalists have long been selectively breeding plants to maximise their yields and usefulness. They have been genetically engineered to grow in hostile conditions and to be resistant to pests and disease, thus maximising yields. Some plants have also been modified in order to produce vaccines.

Factors affecting the rate of photosynthesis

We can measure the rate of photosynthesis by how much oxygen is produced in a given time. Photosynthesis increases and plants grow more during the summer because there is more light and warmth. Three things affect the rate of photosynthesis. We call them '**limiting factors**'. They are:

1 the amount of light
2 the amount of carbon dioxide
3 the temperature.

At any given time one of these factors could be limiting the rate of photosynthesis. In Britain, the rate of photosynthesis is usually limited by the temperature being too low for plants not native to the country. Greenhouses can help maintain a high enough temperature to promote optimum growth conditions. When plants are grown in greenhouses, the amount of carbon dioxide and light can also be maximised.

The leaf

The leaf is the **organ of photosynthesis**. It is an essential organ, without which the plant cannot photosynthesise.

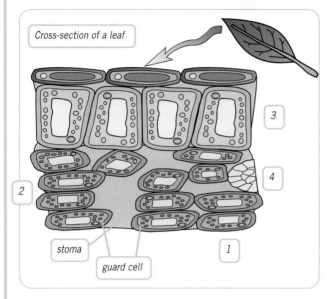

Cross-section of a leaf

2
4
3

stoma

guard cell

1

1 Carbon dioxide enters the leaf through tiny holes on the underside of the leaf by diffusion. These holes are called **stomata** (one = stoma).

2 The **spongy layer** of cells has air spaces for the carbon dioxide to circulate and for the exchange of gases.
- **Oxygen** that is produced by photosynthesis exits by diffusion through the stomata: some is retained for respiration.

3 Chloroplasts are most abundant on the upper surface of the leaf, in **palisade cells**. Chloroplasts contain **chlorophyll**.
- Chlorophyll is a green pigment that **absorbs sunlight** energy.

4 Inside the leaf are **veins**. These veins are continuous with the stem and roots of the plant.
- The veins contain **xylem and phloem**.
- **Xylem** transport **water** from the roots to the leaves.
- **Phloem** transport the **glucose** up and down the plant to wherever it is needed, particularly the growing regions (the bud) and the storage areas (the roots).

> *Make sure you learn about all the substances a plant needs and how they benefit the plant.*

Healthy growth

Minerals are usually present in the soil in quite low concentrations. A method called active transport is used to take them up into root hair cells. Active transport can move substances from a low concentration to a high concentration, against the concentration gradient. It requires energy from respiration to do this.

There are four essential minerals needed for healthy growth:

1 Nitrates are needed for making amino acids, and to form proteins and DNA.
2 Phosphates play an important role in photosynthesis and respiration. Phosphorus is also used for making DNA and cell membranes.
3 Potassium is involved in making the enzymes used in respiration and photosynthesis work.
4 Magnesium is needed in small amounts to make chlorophyll.

A lack of nutrients can cause the following mineral deficiency symptoms:

1 Lack of nitrates causes **stunted growth** and **yellow older leaves**.
2 Lack of phosphates causes **poor root growth** and **purple young leaves**.
3 Lack of potassium causes **yellow leaves with dead spots**.
4 Lack of magnesium causes **yellow leaves**.

> *Try making up a table of minerals a plant needs and why it needs them. Add a column that explains what happens when the plant is deficient in that particular mineral.*

Plant hormones

Plants respond to their surroundings to give them a better chance of survival. Plants' responses are called *tropisms* and are controlled by a *hormone called auxin*. Chemical hormones control the growth of shoots and roots, flowering and the ripening of fruits. A plant's response to *light and gravity* is under the control of auxin.

Control of growth

Plant growth takes place mainly in the **root tip and shoot tip**. The root tip and shoot tip contain hormones called auxins. Auxins move through the plant in solution. They **speed up growth in stems** and **slow down growth in roots**.

> Remember, unequal distribution of auxin creates unequal growth, it speeds up growth in shoots and slows down growth in roots.

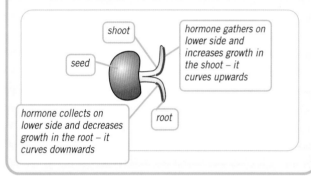

Response to light

A plant's response to light is called **phototropism**. Plants need light to make food during photosynthesis and will grow towards the light, which usually shines from above.

Auxin is spread evenly in the shoot tip, and so the shoot grows upwards.

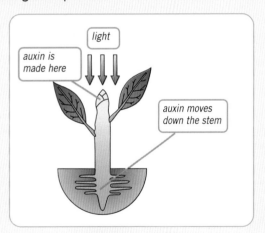

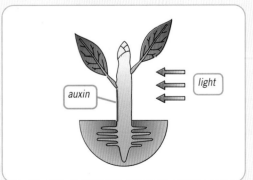

If light comes from one side only, auxin accumulates down the shaded side. The extra auxin makes these cells elongate and grow faster, causing unequal growth.

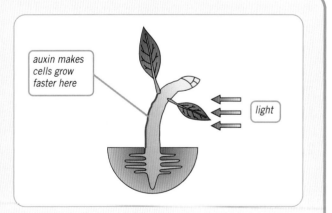

The result is that the shoot bends towards the light. The shoot is described as behaving in a positively phototropic manner.

Response to gravity

A plant's response to gravity is called **geotropism**. Even if you plant a seed the wrong way up the shoot will always grow up, away from gravity; and the root will always grow down, towards gravity. If a plant is put on its side, auxin gathers on the lower half of the shoot and root.

The roots are known as being positively geotropic, and the shoots as being negatively geotropic.

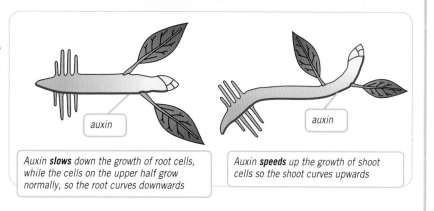

*Auxin **slows** down the growth of root cells, while the cells on the upper half grow normally, so the root curves downwards*

*Auxin **speeds** up the growth of shoot cells so the shoot curves upwards*

Commercial uses of plant hormones

1 Growing cuttings
Rooting powder contains synthetic auxins. A cutting is taken from a plant and dipped in the powder. This stimulates the roots to grow quickly and enables gardeners to grow lots of exact copies of a particular plant.

2 Killing weeds
Synthetic auxins are used as selective weed killers. They only affect broad-leaved weeds: narrow leaved grasses and cereals are not affected. They kill the weed by making the plant grow too fast.

3 Seedless fruits
Synthetic auxins are sprayed on unpollinated flowers. Fruits form without fertilisation and so do not have pips, for example seedless grapes.

4 Early ripening
Plant hormones can also be used to ripen fruit in transport. Bananas are picked when they are unripe and so less easily damaged. By the time they arrive for sale, they are yellow and not green.

 You may be asked to describe ways that plant hormones are used for commercial purposes. Learn the four examples.

1. What is the name of the hormone that controls plants' responses?
2. What is a plant's response to gravity called?
3. What is a plant's response to light called?
4. In which parts of a plant is auxin made?
5. If a light shines onto a plant from the left, on which side will auxin gather?
6. Does auxin speed up or slow down growth in roots?
7. Does auxin speed up or slow down growth in shoots?
8. Name four ways in which plant hormones can be used to benefit gardeners.
9. How does a shoot know which way to grow if it is laid on its side?
10. How does a root know which way to grow if the seed is planted upside down?

Pyramids of numbers and biomass

Before revising pyramids, it is important to remember that a food chain shows us simply who eats who. A food web is a series of linked food chains and gives us a more realistic picture.

Energy enters food chains when plants absorb sunlight during photosynthesis. It is then passed on by animals, feeding. The Sun's energy actually supports all life on Earth. The plants in a food web are known as the *producers* and the animals in the food chain are known as the *consumers*.

Pyramid of numbers

If we look at the information a food chain gives us, it is simply who eats who. A pyramid of numbers tells us how many organisms are involved at each stage of the food chain. At each level of the food chain (called trophic level), the number of organisms generally reduces.

```
      fox
     rabbit
      grass
```

Sometimes, a pyramid of numbers doesn't look like a pyramid at all, as it doesn't take into account the **mass** of the organisms.

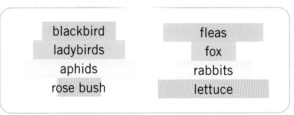

A rose bush counts as one organism but it can support many herbivores. In the pyramid of numbers on the right, the top carnivores are the fleas that feed on a single fox.

Pyramid of biomass

A biomass pyramid takes into account the **mass of each organism** at each level. If we take the information from the pyramid of numbers and multiply it by the organism's mass, we get a pyramid shape again.

```
  blackbird          fleas
  ladybirds           fox
   aphids           rabbits
  rose bush         lettuce
```

A single rose bush weighs more than the aphids, and lots of aphids weigh more than the few ladybirds that feed on them.

A blackbird weighs less than the many ladybirds it feeds on.

Even though there are a lot of fleas, they weigh less than the fox they feed on.

The fox weighs less than the amount of rabbits it eats, and the amount of lettuces the rabbits eat weigh more than the rabbits.

Loss of energy in food chains 1

Food chains rarely have more than four or five links in them. This is because energy is lost along the chain. The final organism only receives a fraction of the energy that was produced at the beginning of the food chain.

Loss of energy in food chains 2

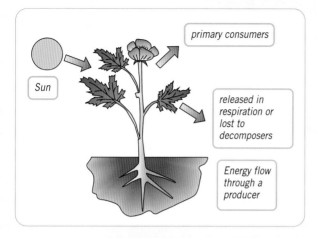

Sun

primary consumers

released in respiration or lost to decomposers

Energy flow through a producer

Plants absorb their energy from the Sun. Only a small fraction of this energy is converted into glucose during photosynthesis. Some energy is lost to decomposers as plants shed their leaves, seeds or fruit.

Only approximately 10% of the original energy from the Sun is passed on to the primary consumer in the plant's biomass.

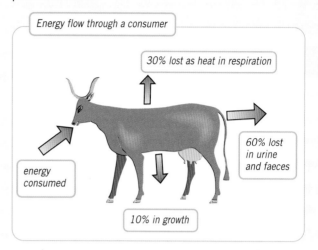

Energy flow through a consumer

30% lost as heat in respiration

60% lost in urine and faeces

energy consumed

10% in growth

Where does the energy go?

The 90% energy loss at each stage goes on life processes such as **respiration and growth**. Respiration **releases heat energy** to the surroundings. Animals that are warm-blooded use up a lot of energy in **keeping warm**. Mammals and birds need to keep their body temperature higher than that of their surroundings and this uses up a lot of energy.

As you can see from the diagram of energy transfers in the cow, a lot of energy is lost in **urine and faeces and not all of the organism's body mass is eaten**.

Exam questions about the energy losses in food chains are common.

Efficiency of energy transfer

Energy is measured in joules. If the amount of energy entering a food chain is 100 joules and only 10 joules is passed on to the primary consumer, then the energy transfer is only 10%.

The calculation is as follows:

$$\text{efficiency \%} = \frac{\text{amount of useful energy after transfer}}{\text{total amount of energy before the transfer}} \times 100$$

QUICK TEST

1. Why do food chains only have four or five links?
2. What do pyramids of numbers show?
3. What don't pyramids of numbers take into account?
4. What is the original energy source of plants?
5. Why do warm-blooded animals lose a lot of energy?
6. List the ways that energy is lost in food chains.

The carbon cycle

Carbon dioxide is a rare, atmospheric gas. It makes up approximately 0.03% of the atmosphere. This amount should stay the same, as the carbon is constantly recycled in what is known as the carbon cycle. The amount of carbon released into the atmosphere balances the amount absorbed by plants. Other nutrients are also recycled in nature.

Parts of the cycle

Photosynthesis

Plants absorb carbon dioxide from the air. They use the carbon to make carbohydrates, proteins and fats, using the **Sun** as an energy source.

Feeding

Animals eat plants and so take the carbon into their bodies to make up their carbohydrates, fats and proteins.

Respiration

Plants, animals and decomposers respire. Respiration releases carbon dioxide back into the atmosphere.

Death and decay

Plants and animals die and produce waste. The carbon is released into the soil.

Decomposers

Bacteria and fungi present in the soil act as decomposers, breaking down dead matter, urine and faeces, which contain carbon. Pieces of dead and decaying material are called detritus. Animals feed on the detritus and help break it down, ready for the decomposers. Microorganisms and detritovores release carbon dioxide when they respire.

Death but no decay

Plants and animals die, but do not always decay. The conditions needed for decay are warmth, moisture and oxygen. If one or more of these conditions are absent when the plant or animal dies, they will not decay. Gradually, over millions of years, heat and pressure change what has not decayed of the animals and plants into fossil fuels.

Fossil fuels

Coal is formed from plants: oil and gas are formed from animals.

Burning and combustion

The burning of fossil fuels (coal, oil and gas) releases carbon dioxide into the atmosphere.

The cycle

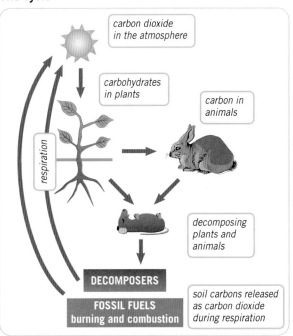

The carbon cycle in the exam may look slightly different. Make sure that you learn all the processes involved.

Remember, there is only one way that carbon enters the cycle (photosynthesis), and two ways that it is released back into the atmosphere (respiration and combustion).

Decomposition and the nutrient cycle

Dead and decaying material (detritus) is first broken down by detritovores such as earthworms, maggots and woodlice. These organisms increase the surface area for bacteria and fungi to completely break the material down.

Bacteria and fungi are **decomposers**. They are also known as **saprophytes**. Saprophytes are organisms that feed by absorbing dead organic matter. Once broken down, the nutrients in the material form part of the soil.

During photosynthesis, plants take up these nutrients, dissolved in water. Animals eat the plants; the animals and plants produce waste and eventually die; and the whole process begins again. This is called the nutrient cycle.

Decomposition happens everywhere in nature. Microorganisms, such as bacteria and fungi, are used to break down compost heaps and sewage. Compost, when rotted down, can be used to help plants grow as it contain nutrients. The ideal conditions for decomposition are **warmth, moisture and oxygen**. Without these factors, decay and decomposition cannot take place.

Microorganisms need oxygen to respire. They also need the temperature to be fairly warm. Bacteria and fungi reproduce in warm temperatures and so the rate of decay would also increase.

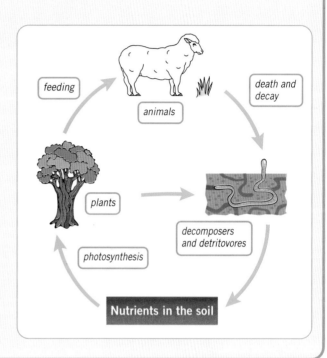

Recycling

It is not just natural elements that can be recycled. Materials like paper, plastics and metals can also be recycled and re-used. Recycling reduces the demand on world resources and the problem of waste disposal.

- Five billion tonnes of paper are sent to landfill each year and yet we import fibres to make paper in order to meet our needs: a process that does not make economic or environmental sense.
- Plastics are made from oil, a non-renewable resource that will one day run out. In 2002, 9.1 billion empty plastic bottles ended up in landfill in the UK, taking up a lot of space. Each year, plastic bottles costing £27 million are disposed of at a cost of £45 million.

Many products can be made from recycled plastic, including fleece jackets. Recycling 25 soft-drink bottles saves enough energy to light a 60 watt light bulb for six hours.

- It is also important to recycle metals. Recycling aluminium saves 95% of the energy needed to make it from its raw materials. In 2000, 42% of aluminium was recycled in the UK, compared with 91% in Switzerland. Steel is 100% recyclable. In the UK, 2.5 billion cans are recycled each year, saving 125,000 tonnes of waste.

Is it worth recycling? What do you think?

1. Name the process by which carbon dioxide is absorbed from the air.

2. What are the two ways that carbon is released back into the air?

3. Name the three types of organisms that carry out respiration.

4. What is 'decomposition'?

5. What organisms are involved in decomposition?

6. What happens to the bodies of animals and plants that do not decay?

7. What are the ideal conditions for decomposition of dead matter to occur?

8. What do the plants do with the carbon they absorb?

The nitrogen cycle

The atmosphere contains 78% of nitrogen gas. Nitrogen is an important element needed for making *proteins*. Plants and animals cannot use nitrogen in this form. It has to be *converted into nitrates* before plants can use it to make protein. We eat plants and ingest the protein into our bodies. It is a continuous cycle and so can begin anywhere. *Nitrogen gas is changed into nitrates in the nitrogen cycle.*

The nitrogen cycle 1

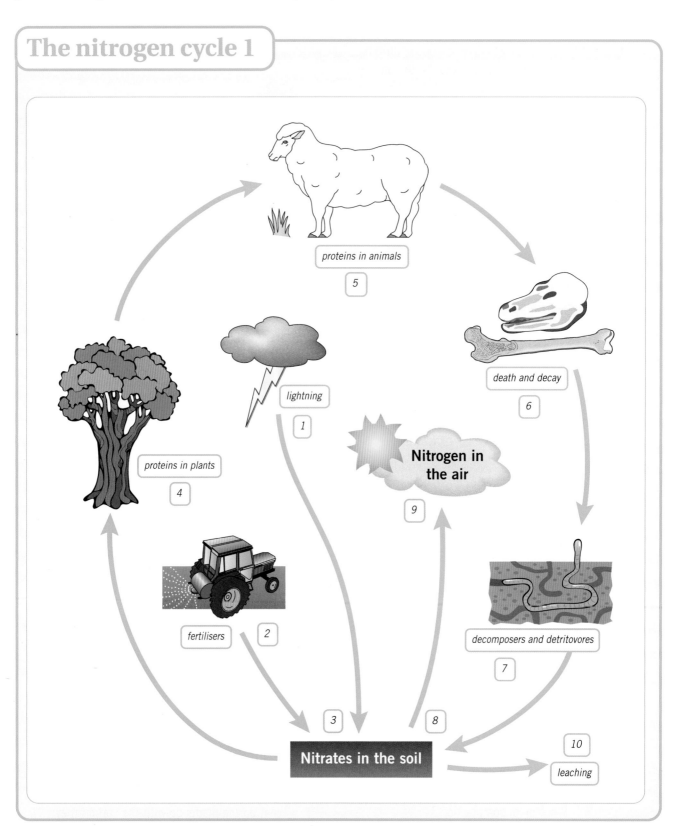

proteins in animals
5

lightning
1

death and decay
6

proteins in plants
4

Nitrogen in the air
9

fertilisers
2

decomposers and detritovores
7

3   8

Nitrates in the soil

10
leaching

The nitrogen cycle 2

The numbered points below relate to the numbers on the diagram of the nitrogen cycle, so you can see what happens at each stage.

1 **Lightning** causes the nitrogen and oxygen to combine to form nitrogen oxides. These dissolve in rain and are washed into the soil to form **nitrates** in the soil.
2 Fertilisers can be added to the soil to improve the **nitrate** content.
3 **Nitrogen-fixing bacteria** in the soil convert nitrogen from the air into **nitrates**. Nitrogen-fixing bacteria in the roots of some leguminous plants – like peas, beans and clover – also change nitrogen into **nitrates**. The bacteria form lumps, called **root nodules**.

4 Plants take up the **nitrates** from the soil and convert them into **proteins**.

5 **Animals eat the plants** and take the protein into their bodies, where it becomes a part of the animal's protein.
6 Animals and plants produce waste and eventually die. After death, their bodies decay.
7 **Detritovores** – such as worms, maggots and woodlice – feed on dead and decaying material, making it easier for decomposers to break it down.

Decomposers, such as fungi and bacteria, turn this material into ammonium compounds that contain nitrogen.
8 **Nitrifying bacteria** in the soil change **ammonia into nitrates**.
9 **Denitrifying bacteria** live in waterlogged soils: they can change **nitrates** back into ammonia and nitrogen gas that is returned to the atmosphere.
10 **Nitrates** can be washed out of the soil before plants take them up. This is called **leaching**, and can have serious consequences for rivers and streams.

> *There are four ways in which nitrogen is converted into nitrates in the soil and two ways in which nitrates are taken out of the soil.*

Summary

- Lightning, artificial fertilisers and nitrogen-fixing bacteria in the soil and in root nodules convert nitrogen into nitrates.
- Nitrifying bacteria in the soil change animal waste and dead remains into ammonia and, eventually, nitrates.
- Denitrifying bacteria live in waterlogged soils and convert nitrates back into nitrogen.

> *Make sure you know the three types of bacteria involved in the nitrogen cycle.*

QUICK TEST

1. What do plants need nitrates for?
2. What does nitrogen have to be converted to before it can be used?
3. What part does lightning play in the nitrogen cycle?
4. Where are nitrogen-fixing bacteria found?
5. Where are nitrifying bacteria found and what do they do?
6. What are denitrifying bacteria?
7. What is another way that nitrates can be taken out of the soil?
8. Why are leguminous plants good for the soil?
9. What happens to the waste and dead remains of plants and animals?
10. Where do animals get their protein from?

Enzymes and digestion

The digestive system is really one long tube called the gut. Digestion begins with the teeth and ends at the anus.

Enzymes have many uses, particularly in speeding up the process of digestion.

Digestion

Physical digestion begins with the teeth breaking food into smaller pieces by chewing and also the churning in the stomach. Chemical digestion involves enzymes working outside of body cells.

Digestion is the breaking down of large insoluble molecules into small soluble molecules so that they can be absorbed into the blood stream.

The large insoluble molecules are starch, protein and fat. This action is speeded up (catalysed) by enzymes. Enzymes are found throughout the digestive system.

Food does not pass through the pancreas, liver and gall bladder. They are organs that secrete enzymes and bile to help digestion.

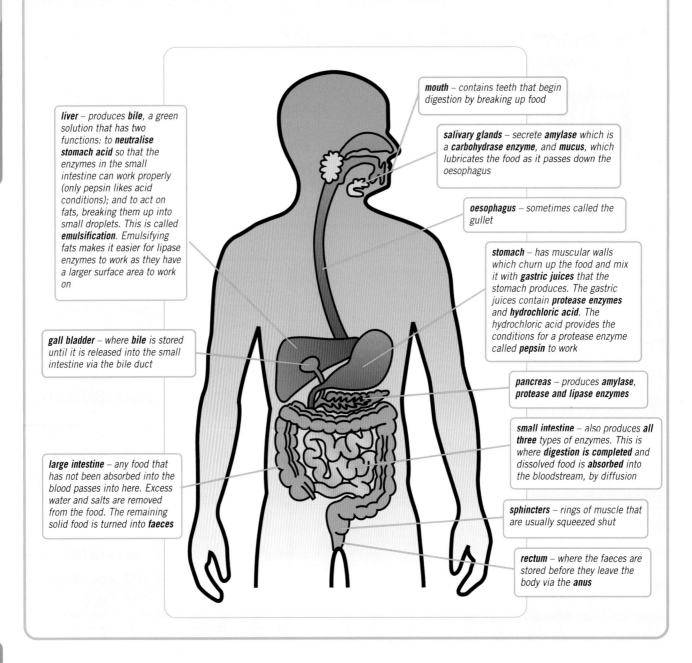

liver – produces **bile**, a green solution that has two functions: to **neutralise stomach acid** so that the enzymes in the small intestine can work properly (only pepsin likes acid conditions); and to act on fats, breaking them up into small droplets. This is called **emulsification**. Emulsifying fats makes it easier for lipase enzymes to work as they have a larger surface area to work on

gall bladder – where **bile** is stored until it is released into the small intestine via the bile duct

large intestine – any food that has not been absorbed into the blood passes into here. Excess water and salts are removed from the food. The remaining solid food is turned into **faeces**

mouth – contains teeth that begin digestion by breaking up food

salivary glands – secrete **amylase** which is a **carbohydrase enzyme**, and **mucus**, which lubricates the food as it passes down the oesophagus

oesophagus – sometimes called the gullet

stomach – has muscular walls which churn up the food and mix it with **gastric juices** that the stomach produces. The gastric juices contain **protease enzymes** and **hydrochloric acid**. The hydrochloric acid provides the conditions for a protease enzyme called **pepsin** to work

pancreas – produces **amylase**, **protease** and **lipase** enzymes

small intestine – also produces **all three** types of enzymes. This is where **digestion is completed** and dissolved food is **absorbed** into the bloodstream, by diffusion

sphincters – rings of muscle that are usually squeezed shut

rectum – where the faeces are stored before they leave the body via the **anus**

Enzymes speed things up

Starch, protein and fats are **large, insoluble food** molecules. Enzymes are needed to break them down into **small, soluble molecules**. If you look back at the diagram of the digestive system you will see where these **chemicals, called enzymes**, are made. Enzymes are specific. There are **three main enzymes** in your system.

Starch is broken down into glucose in the mouth and small intestine. Proteins are broken down into amino acids in the stomach and the small intestine. Fats are broken down into fatty acids and glycerol in the small intestine.

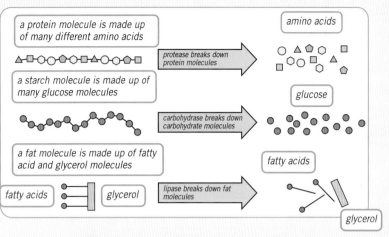

a protein molecule is made up of many different amino acids

protease breaks down protein molecules

amino acids

a starch molecule is made up of many glucose molecules

carbohydrase breaks down carbohydrate molecules

glucose

a fat molecule is made up of fatty acid and glycerol molecules

fatty acids   *glycerol*

lipase breaks down fat molecules

fatty acids

glycerol

💡 *Each part of the digestive system has a particular job. Learn the functions of each of the parts and where the enzymes and other helpful secretions are produced.*

What are enzymes and how do they work?

Enzymes are proteins made up of long chains of amino acids. Each enzyme is folded into a specific shape, which allows other molecules to fit into it. The other molecules are called substrates. The enzyme and the substrate fit together using a **lock and key** mechanism. The enzyme has an **active site**.

Enzymes are called **biological catalysts**. They speed up biological reactions inside and outside of body cells, such as respiration, protein synthesis, photosynthesis and digestion. Enzyme activity is affected by pH and temperature, and each enzyme has its own, **optimum** conditions.

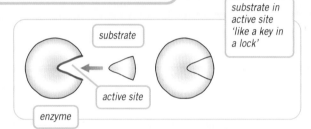

substrate

active site

enzyme

substrate in active site 'like a key in a lock'

At too low a temperature, the rate at which the substrate joins with the enzyme's active site is slowed down and so the reaction is slower.

At too high a temperature or extremes of pH, the enzyme becomes denatured: this means that the active site is distorted and the reaction no longer occurs.

Uses of enzymes in the home and industry

Enzymes are cheap to use in industry and the home. They do not require high temperatures to work and can be reused.

Biological washing powders contain enzymes produced by bacteria, such as proteases and lipases, to digest fats and protein stains on clothes. **In industry**, carbohydrases are used in the making of chocolate and

syrup, and proteases are used to pre-digest the protein in baby food. Isomerase is used to convert glucose syrup into the much sweeter fructose syrup, which is used in smaller quantities in slimming foods.

💡 *Make sure that you know how enzymes work. Remember that they are specific to a substrate and have an optimum pH and temperature at which they work best.*

QUICK TEST

1. Where is the enzyme amylase produced?
2. What are the functions of bile?
3. Where in the digestive system does the food get absorbed into the blood stream?
4. What are the soluble products of fat digestion?
5. What are enzymes made up of?
6. What factors affect how enzymes work?
7. Give an example of how proteases are used in industry.

Respiration and exercise

Respiration is the *breakdown of glucose to make energy using oxygen.*

Every living cell, in every living organism, uses respiration to make energy, all of the time. Energy is needed for all the chemical reactions that take place in the body. Most of the chemical reactions involved in respiration take place inside the mitochondria of a cell's cytoplasm.

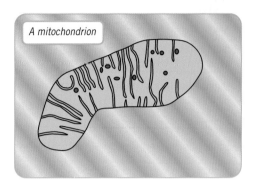
A mitochondrion

Exercise and fitness

During exercise, respiration in the muscles increases; breathing and heart rate also increase, in order to deliver oxygen and glucose to the muscles more quickly and remove carbon dioxide more quickly. An increase in heart rate and breathing rate is normal during exercise – how much they increase during and after exercise can indicate a person's fitness. One way of measuring fitness is to look at a person's recovery time after exercise. The process is as follows:

■ Take a **pulse rate** before exercise (the resting rate) for 15 seconds, then multiply by four to get the rate per minute. The best place to take a reading is on the carotid artery in the neck or the radial artery on the underside of the wrist.

■ Exercise, perhaps by running on the spot, for two minutes.

■ Take the pulse rate again immediately after exercise and then every minute, until the pulse returns to the resting rate.

■ The time it takes for the pulse rate to return to the resting rate is known as the 'recovery time' or **recovery rate**.

■ A fit person will recover much faster than an unfit person. An unfit person is also more likely to have a higher pulse rate before, during and after exercise.

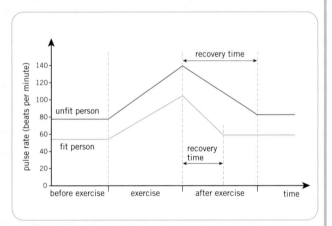

Breathing rate and heart rate monitors can also be worn on the wrist or around the body near the heart. They provide a far more accurate way of taking measurements than by hand because they produce a continuous measurement before, during and after exercise. Monitors also reduce the chance of human error in the readings.

Aerobic respiration and exercise

Aerobic respiration provides energy for the body to do work. During exercise, breathing and pulse rates increase. The arteries supplying the muscles also dilate in order to deliver oxygen and glucose more quickly to the respiring muscles and to remove carbon dioxide more quickly. The blood transports the glucose and oxygen and takes carbon dioxide away. Aerobic means 'with air' and, as respiration requires oxygen, we call it **aerobic respiration**.

The chemical equation for respiration is:

$$C_6H_{12}O_6 + 6O_2 \rightarrow 6CO_2 + 6H_2O + \textbf{ENERGY}$$

The word equation is:

glucose + oxygen $\rightarrow$ carbon dioxide + water + **ENERGY**

It is important to learn both the word and chemical equation for respiration.

Uses of the energy produced

Energy produced during respiration is used for:

- making your muscles work – your muscles contain a lot of mitochondria, as they need a lot of energy during exercise
- absorbing molecules against concentration gradients, a process called active transport
- chemical reactions

- the growth and repair of cells
- making up larger molecules from smaller ones, such as proteins from amino acids
- maintaining body temperature in warm-blooded animals, such as mammals and birds
- building up sugars, nitrates and other nutrients into amino acids in plants, which are then further built up into proteins.

Dieting and health

Advice on exercise and **diet** changes regularly. It is thought that exercising three times a week for 20 minutes is enough to maintain the good health of most people, although this will vary from person to person.

There are many different types of diets on the market for people to follow, but the question is, are they safe? What is a healthy diet? Opinions vary greatly. The general consensus is that a healthy diet is a balanced diet that matches energy intake with the amount of energy used up during exercise.

It is important to note that the health benefits of losing weight for those who are overweight are crucial. A doctor's advice should, however, always be sought before embarking on any type of diet as your health may be put at risk, particularly when embarking on a so-called 'fad' or fashionable diet.

Fashionable diets – the Atkins diet

The **Atkins diet** is based on the theory that when we eat carbohydrates and sugar, the body converts them to fat that is then stored. The diet aims to use fats and proteins as an energy source, as opposed to carbohydrates. This may lead to an initial weight loss, probably because eating a high fat diet is more satisfying for longer, so reducing the urge to snack or overindulge when hungry. Any weight loss will soon level out.

There are a number of health problems associated with this diet. The lack of fruit and vegetables, which contain fibre and keep constipation at bay, can be an issue. The main health concern is the long-term effect of all the fat and cholesterol consumed. These fats clog up the arteries and can lead to heart disease and strokes. Furthermore, the damage is difficult to reverse. Eating a diet high in protein also puts strain on the liver, which must break the protein down. The urea produced from the breakdown of protein then puts pressure on the kidneys, which must then remove the increased amount of urea in the urine.

QUICK TEST

1. Define 'aerobic respiration'.
2. What are the waste products of respiration?
3. Where does respiration take place?
4. What does the term 'recovery rate' mean?
5. Why are heart rate monitors more reliable than taking a pulse by hand?
6. What organs are put under strain by a high protein diet?
7. Why does the breathing rate increase with exercise?
8. Why does the pulse rate increase with exercise?

Blood and blood vessels

Blood is a fluid that transports food and oxygen to cells and removes waste products. It consists of *red blood cells, white blood cells* and *platelets*, suspended in a fluid called *plasma*. The heart provides the force to pump the blood around the body.

Red blood cells

The function of **red blood cells** is to **carry oxygen** to all the cells of the body.

- They have **no nucleus**, meaning that there is more room for haemoglobin.
- They are **small** and **flexible**, in order to pass through small blood vessels.
- They are shaped as **small biconcave discs**, providing maximum surface area to volume ratio for absorbing oxygen.
- They contain a substance called **haemoglobin**. In the lungs this substance combines with oxygen to form

This diagram shows a red blood cell that has been sectioned to show its characteristic shape

oxyhaemoglobin. In the tissues it gives up the oxygen to form haemoglobin again.

oxygen + haemoglobin ⇌ oxyhaemoglobin

 Learn the functions of the four parts of the blood and, in particular, how the structure of the red blood cell is adapted to its function.

White blood cells

The main function of white blood cells is defence against disease.

- They have a large nucleus.
- They are larger than red blood cells and their shape varies.
- They have a flexible shape, in order to engulf microorganisms.

Phagocytes
this type of white blood cell kills microbes by ingesting them

Lymphocytes
this type of white blood cell sends out antibodies which kill microbes

There are two main types of white blood cells that can multiply if needed.

Platelets

Platelets are fragments of cells. Their function is to **clot the blood** so you do not bleed to death if you cut yourself.

Plasma

Plasma is a yellow fluid. It consists mainly of water with many substances dissolved in it. These substances include soluble food, salts, carbon dioxide, urea, hormones, antibodies and plasma proteins. Its function is to **transport these substances** around the body.

Blood vessels 1

Veins
Veins carry **deoxygenated** blood, blood that has given up its oxygen to the body tissues. They carry the blood **back to the heart** from the body at low pressure. They

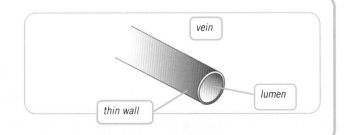

vein

lumen

thin wall

Blood vessels 2

have **valves** to prevent the blood flowing backwards. Veins have a large **lumen**, or hole, in the middle.

Arteries

Arteries carry **oxygenated** blood. They carry blood **away from the heart**, towards the body, at **high pressure**. They have very **thick, muscular, elastic walls** to withstand the high pressure. The high pressure in the arteries causes **a pulse** that can be felt in the wrist and neck.

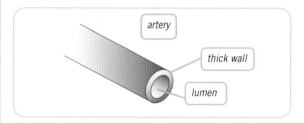

Capillaries

Capillaries are only **one cell thick** and have very thin, permeable walls, to allow oxygen and nutrients to diffuse out of them. When something is permeable, it has tiny holes in it that allow small substances to flow through. These capillaries are the site of exchange between the blood and the cells of the body.

Fluid leaks out of the capillaries and bathes the surrounding cells. This is called **tissue fluid**. The tissue fluid delivers the food and oxygen to the cells and receives waste products, which are reabsorbed back into the capillaries.

> *It is worth knowing the structural differences between arteries, veins and capillaries, and how this structure relates to their functions.*

The heart

The heart consists of a special type of muscle called cardiac muscle. It contracts continuously without getting tired. The heart is a double pump. The left side pumps oxygenated blood out of the aorta at high pressure to other arteries, to deliver substances around the body. The right side of the heart carries deoxygenated blood and pumps it to the lungs to be oxygenated.

The left side of the heart has much thicker walls, as it has to pump blood at high pressure all the way around the body. The top two chambers of the heart are called atria (the singular of which is atrium). They receive blood from the body and the lungs. The bottom two chambers of the heart are called ventricles. They pump the blood out of the heart.

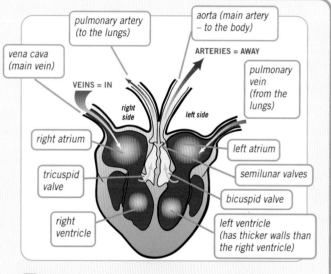

> *Make sure that you learn the names of all the major blood vessels entering and leaving the heart.*

QUICK TEST

1. Which side of the heart contains deoxygenated blood?
2. Name two blood vessels that enter the heart.
3. Name two blood vessels that leave the heart.
4. What are the semilunar valves for?
5. Name the substance in red blood cells that combines with oxygen.
6. Why do arteries have elastic, muscular walls?
7. Which blood vessel contains valves?
8. Which blood vessels are the site of exchange of substances between the blood and the body?

Manipulating life

The manipulation of genes can take many forms: from the selective breeding of animals and plants, to attempting to cure diseases by gene therapy.

The modification of genes – 'genetic modification' – is not without controversy.

Selective breeding

Selective breeding is the process whereby man breeds the desired features into a plant or animal and breeds out those features that are not wanted. As humans do the selecting, rather than nature, we call it **artificial selection**. Farmers can also use selective breeding to increase the number of offspring from farm animals, to increase yields from plants, and produce better quality plants and animals.

Animals, however, can only breed using sexual reproduction, which always produces some variation in the offspring. It is easier to selectively breed plants, because it is relatively simple to clone a plant. Clones are genetically identical individuals produced by asexual reproduction. Asexual reproduction involves only one parent.

Cloning plants is much easier than cloning animals because plant cells are able to differentiate (specialise into many different types of cells) throughout their life: animal cells lose this ability at an early stage. Plants grown from cuttings are an example of cloning.

Tissue culture

Tissue culture is a technique used by commercial plant breeders.

The advantage of this process is that new plants with special properties, such as resistance to diseases, can be grown quickly and cheaply all year round.

Plants that are difficult to grow from seed can be mass produced using this method. Each plant will be identical to the original and so the grower can be sure of its characteristics.

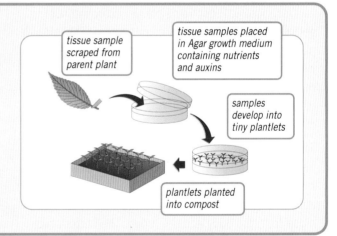

tissue sample scraped from parent plant

tissue samples placed in Agar growth medium containing nutrients and auxins

samples develop into tiny plantlets

plantlets planted into compost

Dolly the sheep

Dolly the sheep was the first mammal to be cloned, in 1996. She died prematurely in 2003. The procedure used to create her is shown on the right.

Dolly's early death fuelled the debate about the long-term health problems of clones. Many cloned animals died even before their embryos were implanted. Scientists discovered that these embryos had an 'inappropriate expression' of genes. This would have led to a number of deformities if the embryos had been successfully implanted and, in all likelihood, they would not have reached full term.

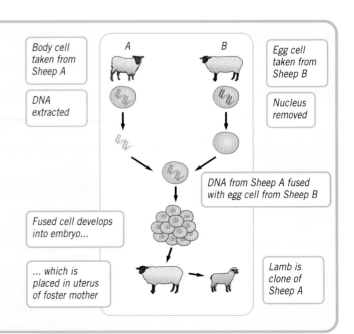

Body cell taken from Sheep A

DNA extracted

A

B

Egg cell taken from Sheep B

Nucleus removed

DNA from Sheep A fused with egg cell from Sheep B

Fused cell develops into embryo...

... which is placed in uterus of foster mother

Lamb is clone of Sheep A

Genetic modification

Over the past 20 years there have been huge developments in **genetic modification (GM) technology**, but a great deal remains undiscovered. The completion of the human genome (human DNA) and that of other plants and animals have also increased the possibilities of research.

The benefits of genetically modifying crops are that crop characteristics can be improved very quickly, leading to resistance to pests and herbicides. Plants can also be manipulated to produce artificial substances like oral vaccines. More recent advances include plants that can tolerate drought and other hostile conditions, and the development of crops that are tastier or more nutritious.

The risks involved in genetically modifying crops include the possibility of allergic reactions and the chance that pest and herbicide resistance will spread to wild varieties of crops and weeds. There is also concern that the control of agriculture is moving towards biotechnology corporations and away from farmers.

Some people argue that genetic modification is both safe and necessary, in order to match population growth and help feed the millions in third world countries more effectively. Others argue that there is more than enough food being produced globally and that the problem lies with the distribution, not production, of food.

Another fear is that GM crops will reduce biodiversity. If crops are made resistant to herbicides, and the fields are then treated with herbicides to kill the weeds, other species that rely on the weeds for food would also die out. The growing of insect-resistant crops would also reduce the number of insects, and so have an impact on many food chains.

One argument for GM crops states that it is really no different from artificial selection by humans: they are both forms of genetic engineering.

Gene therapy

Gene therapy is a technique for correcting defective genes responsible for disease development. In most studies, a viral vector carrying a 'normal' gene is inserted into the patient's cells to replace an 'abnormal', disease-causing gene.

Research is ongoing into all types of gene therapy. At present, human gene therapy products are not yet on the market, as human gene therapy is still experimental and has not proved to be a success in most clinical trials. As a treatment for cancer, however, it is proving to be more promising. **Gene therapy may be used to treat cancer** in the following ways.

- Specially made genes could be put into the cancer cells to make them more sensitive than normal cells to treatments such as chemotherapy.
- Genes could be added into cancer cells and then activated, to produce a poisonous substance (toxin) that kills the cell.
- Genes could be introduced into cancer cells that make those cells more obvious to the body's own defences (the immune system) so that they are destroyed 'naturally' by the immune system.
- Damaged genes could be replaced by versions that work correctly.
- New genes could be put into normal cells to make them more resistant to the side effects of treatment, such as radiotherapy and chemotherapy. This would protect the normal cells from the treatments so that higher doses could be given.

There are two types of gene therapy: one focuses on treating the patient; and the other on eggs and sperm, with the intention of preventing the occurrence of some inherited diseases. Preventing disease in this way has great potential but is controversial, and very little research is conducted in this area for ethical reasons, as you are affecting not just that patient but the future generations they may produce.

QUICK TEST

1. What is 'gene therapy'?
2. What is GM an abbreviation for?
3. Who was Dolly the sheep?
4. Give another term for selective breeding.
5. What is a 'clone'?
6. How could genetically modifying plants affect food chains?
7. What are the advantages of growing plants by tissue culture?

Mendel and genetics

Genetics is the study of how information is passed on from generation to generation. Genetic diagrams are used to show how certain characteristics are passed on.

Mendel's experiments

For thousands of years farmers had been selectively breeding animals and plants to produce more useful ones. This was largely hit or miss since the processes controlling inheritance was unknown.

Gregor Mendel, an Austrian monk and teacher who carried out basic genetics research in his spare time, discovered the principle behind genetics by studying the inheritance of a single factor in pea plants. The inheritance of single characteristics is called **monohybrid inheritance**. The importance of his discoveries was not recognised until after his death in 1884. The development of microscopes in 1890 also enabled scientists to discover the basics of cell division and sexual reproduction. This led them to focus on what really happens with the inheritance of characteristics from parents to children.

Mendel chose pea plants because they could easily be manipulated and grew quickly. Pea plants possess both male and female reproductive organs and so could self-pollinate or cross-pollinate with another plant. He bred a **pure breeding, red pea plant with a pure breeding, white pea plant** and found that they always produced red flowers (**the F1 generation**). He named the red feature the **dominant** characteristic. When he bred two of the red pea plants together, he discovered that the next set of flowers were a mixture of red and white pea flowers (**the F2 generation**). The **ratio** of red to white flowers was **3:1**. Mendel called the white characteristic, **recessive**.

From his experiments, Mendel concluded that the peas must carry a **pair of factors for each feature**. When the seeds were formed, they inherited one factor at random from each parent. We now call these factors, **genes**. Genes occur on **pairs of chromosomes** and each form of a gene is called an **allele**. Mendel also came to the conclusion that a characteristic may not show up in an individual but can still be passed on.

We can show the results of Mendel's pea plant cross using symbols.

The **dominant** characteristic is given a **capital letter** and the **recessive** characteristic a **lower case letter**. In this example, 'R' represents red flowers and 'r' represents white flowers.

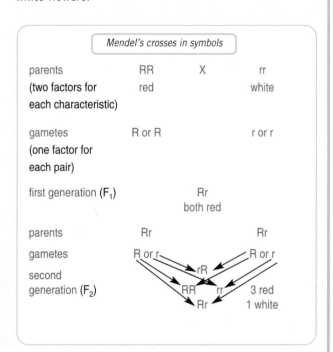

Definitions 1

Chromosomes are contained inside the nucleus of a cell. Genes are found on chromosomes.

A **gene** is a unit of inheritance. We have a pair of genes for each feature.

Alleles are alternative forms of a gene: for example, the gene for pea plant colour has two alleles, red and white.

Recessive means it is the weaker allele that will only have an effect in the homozygous recessive condition.

Dominant means it is the stronger allele that will have an effect in the heterozygous condition.

The **genotype** is the type of alleles an organism carries.

Definitions 2

The genotype of the red pea plants could be RR or Rr. Although the genotypes are different, they are still red because red is dominant.

The **phenotype** is what the plant physically looks like, and is the result of what genotype the organism has.

If an organism has two identical alleles, they are **homozygous dominant** (RR) or **homozygous recessive** (rr).

If an organism has different alleles, they are **heterozygous** (Rr).

Gametes are the sex cells (sperm or egg), formed by **meiosis**, that contain half the genetic information (**genes**).

It is essential that you learn all these definitions to understand genetics.

Scientific concept

Charles Darwin, whose theory of evolution is accepted today, lived around the same time as Gregor Mendel but never saw his research. He would have been one of the few scientists to understand Mendel's work.

Inheritance of coat colour in mice

What happens if you cross a homozygous grey mouse with a homozygous white mouse?

In this case, we can represent the grey allele with the letter 'G' and the white allele with the letter 'g'.

All the offspring are grey, which means that grey was the dominant characteristic.

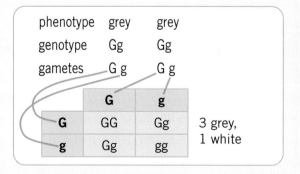

phenotype	grey	white
genotype	GG	gg
gametes	G G	g g

	g	**g**
G	Gg	Gg
G	Gg	Gg

all grey, all Gg

If two heterozygous mice were crossed, the outcome would be as follows:

phenotype	grey	grey
genotype	Gg	Gg
gametes	G g	G g

	G	**g**
G	GG	Gg
g	Gg	gg

3 grey, 1 white

The white mice must have the genotype 'gg', but the grey mouse could have genotype GG or Gg. We can't tell simply by looking at it. To find out you could cross the grey mouse with another white mouse (with the genotype gg). If any of the offspring are white, the grey mouse must be heterozygous (Gg). If they are all grey, the grey mouse must be homozygous (GG). This is called a test cross. **Remember that these ratios are only probabilities and may not always occur.**

If you have to choose letters to represent dominant and recessive characteristics, make sure you choose letters that look noticeably different, such as R and r, not S and s.

QUICK TEST

1. What was the dominant characteristic in Mendel's experiments?
2. What does 'recessive' mean?
3. What do we now call the factors for each feature?
4. What is monohybrid inheritance?
5. What is a 'phenotype'?
6. What does pure breeding mean?
7. If an organism has two identical alleles, is it homozygous or heterozygous?
8. What sort of test could you conduct to find out the genotype of an individual?

Growth

Growth is an irreversible increase in the size or mass of an organism. The growth processes in animals include cell division by *mitosis* and *differentiation*, where cells become specialised for their purpose. Growth involves changes of shape as well as size.

Human growth

Each particular species of animal has a size range. For example, different breeds of dogs, such as dachshunds and Great Danes, vary greatly in height, as do the Great Danes themselves.

The height range of human beings is known as a continuous variable. It is influenced by a number of genes as many different heights lie in-between the extremes.

Height is also influenced by nutrition (humans are smaller when they are undernourished); and by

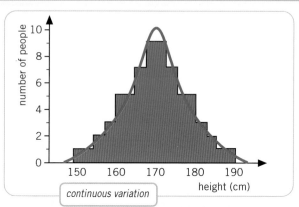

continuous variation

hormones such as the growth hormone produced by the pituitary gland in the brain.

Measuring growth

Growth can be measured by:
■ looking at the increase in length and height of organisms
■ measuring the mass of organisms, live, wet mass or dry mass.

It is difficult to measure the live mass of aquatic organisms simply because they are in water. We need to be sure we are measuring the organism but none of

the water, so we need to ask: how much of the mass is water on the surface of the animal? and how much do you dry them out? Live mass is not an entirely accurate measure of mass where terrestrial animals are concerned either, as they too may be holding excess water. A measure of dry mass can be used for all organisms, but the animals have to be dead and dried out in an oven first.

The Hayflick Limit

The **Hayflick Limit** is named after the man who made a discovery about cell division. He observed cells dividing in the human lungs and noticed that they only divided about 50 times before they died. As cells approached this limit, they exhibited signs of old age. This limit has been observed in all human cell types that have been fully differentiated. It varies from cell to cell, and from organism to organism, but the human limit of cell division is around 52 times.

Exceptions

Stem cells are cells in the body that have not yet been fully differentiated. They are found in embryos and in some adult cells, such as the bone marrow. Stem cells continue to divide and regenerate throughout the organism's life. When cells grow out of control, the result is cancer. The Hayflick Limit may exist to prevent **cancer**. When cells reach the Hayflick Limit, any tumour formed would no longer be able to divide and so would then die off. The problem is that some cancers have found ways around the Hayflick Limit and become 'immortal', malignant tumours.

Regeneration

Regeneration is the ability to re-grow parts of the body. Only certain animals can do this: they include some spiders, worms and reptiles. Lizards can also re-grow their tails if they lose them in a fight. These animals have cells that are able to revert back from being specialised cells to undifferentiated cells that then re-specialise.

Growth factors in sport

Growth factors include anabolic steroids, HGH (human growth hormone) and EPO (erythropoietin). Athletes use growth factors to enhance their performance in sport despite the fact that they carry many health risks and are classed by many as cheating.

Anabolic steroids can cause high blood pressure, acne, abnormalities in liver function, kidney failure, heart disease, changes in the menstrual cycle in women and a decline in sperm production and impotence in men. They also make both sexes more aggressive.

There is a problem with detecting these growth factors, as many are similar to substances produced naturally in the body. New tests are being developed that can tell the difference between these substances.

Factors affecting growth

The inheritance of genes in a plant will determine growth: for example, there are tall and dwarf varieties of wheat plants and pea plants. There are also different shaped plants: for example, potatoes and runner beans.

Environmental factors also play an important part in plant growth. Plants are influenced a great deal by the climate and availability of nutrients. Light, carbon dioxide and water are essential for photosynthesis and life, and therefore growth. In areas where these factors are lacking, such as the desert (water) and in the shade (light), very few plants are able to grow. A plant grown in sunlight will develop much more rapidly and may soon be double the size of a comparative plant grown in the shade. In woodlands, the tallest plants are the trees, which grow towards the light. Their leaves create a canopy that restricts the amount of light that reaches the ground. As a result, plants on the floor of the woodland are few and far between. They tend to be hardy plant types, like ferns, that can survive with less light.

Scientific concept

The limit of cell division is believed to be one of the causes of ageing. It is linked to the shortening of a region of DNA at the ends of chromosomes. If this can be slowed down or prevented, life expectancy could be extended. There is a great deal of research currently being conducted in this area.

Growth in plants

Plants grow in a similar way to animals, through cell division by mitosis and cell differentiation. They also undergo a process called elongation, whereby the cell vacuole absorbs water and swells.

A plant's root tip and shoot are the only areas capable of cell division: the rest of the plant grows by elongation and cell differentiation. Unlike animal cells, plant cells retain the ability to differentiate throughout their life.

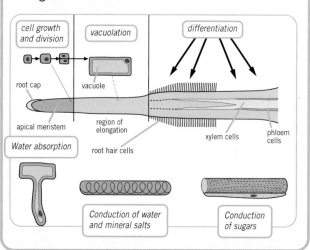

QUICK TEST

1. What is meant by the term 'Hayflick Limit'?
2. What type of cell has no Hayflick Limit?
3. What are growth factors in sport?
4. How do animals grow from a fertilised egg cell?
5. What does 'regeneration' mean?
6. Which parts of a plant are capable of cell division?

Mitosis

How do we grow from a fertilised egg? How do we replace cells when we have cut ourselves? The answer to both these questions is through a process of cell division called *mitosis*. It produces all cells, except the sex cells. *Mitosis occurs in the growth and replacement of cells.*

Mitosis

When a cell divides and reproduces to produce **two daughter cells that are identical to the original parent cell**, this process is known as mitosis.

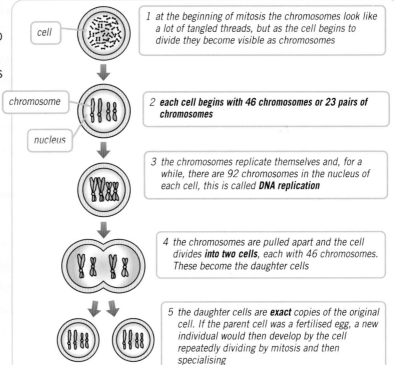

1 at the beginning of mitosis the chromosomes look like a lot of tangled threads, but as the cell begins to divide they become visible as chromosomes

2 **each cell begins with 46 chromosomes or 23 pairs of chromosomes**

3 the chromosomes replicate themselves and, for a while, there are 92 chromosomes in the nucleus of each cell, this is called **DNA replication**

4 the chromosomes are pulled apart and the cell divides **into two cells**, each with 46 chromosomes. These become the daughter cells

5 the daughter cells are **exact** copies of the original cell. If the parent cell was a fertilised egg, a new individual would then develop by the cell repeatedly dividing by mitosis and then specialising

DNA replication

Just before a cell begins to divide, the chromosomes have to be duplicated. The chromosomes are made up of long strands of deoxyribonucleic acid, DNA for short. **DNA has the ability to copy itself exactly.**

There is no need to learn the names of the bases in DNA.

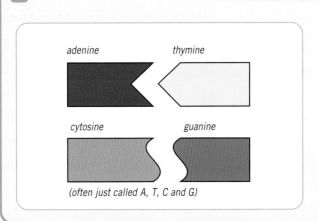

adenine   thymine

cytosine   guanine

(often just called A, T, C and G)

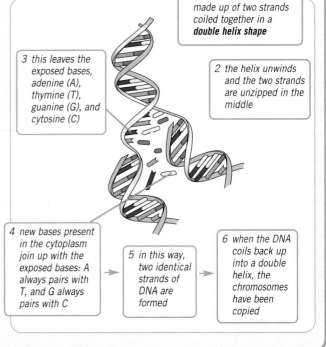

1 the DNA molecule is made up of two strands coiled together in a **double helix shape**

2 the helix unwinds and the two strands are unzipped in the middle

3 this leaves the exposed bases, adenine (A), thymine (T), guanine (G), and cytosine (C)

4 new bases present in the cytoplasm join up with the exposed bases: A always pairs with T, and G always pairs with C

5 in this way, two identical strands of DNA are formed

6 when the DNA coils back up into a double helix, the chromosomes have been copied

Mitosis and asexual reproduction

There are two types of reproduction, **sexual reproduction** and asexual reproduction.

Asexual reproduction involves only **one parent**. The offspring have exact copies of the parent's genes and are called clones.

Asexual reproduction uses mitosis to produce clones.

Sexual reproduction involves fertilisation and produces offspring that are not genetically identical. Sexual reproduction always involves a male and a female gamete, produced by meiosis.

 Learn the difference between asexual reproduction and sexual reproduction.

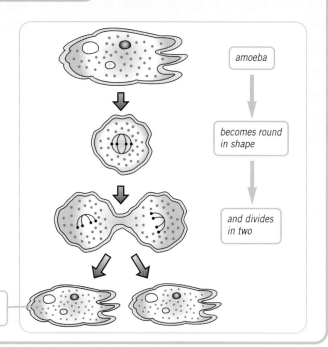

amoeba

becomes round in shape

and divides in two

asexual reproduction by an amoeba

Stem cell therapy

Stem cell therapy is ongoing research into the treatment of human disease and organ failure. Stem cells are cells that have the ability to replicate and specialise into different types of tissue. They are found in adult bone marrow, human embryos and the umbilical cord. Adult stem cells do not have the same potential as embryonic stem cells to treat illness.

Stem cells have the ability to divide and specialise into any tissue needed, such as nerve cells. Treatment with these cells may help conditions such as paralysis.

Stem cell therapy research and use is still in its early stages. It requires much more funding, support and regulation, particularly when the stem cells involved are from donated human embryos. There are ethical questions to be asked whether or not it is legally or morally right to experiment on a human embryo created by IVF.

The potential for stem cell therapy is endless. Stem cells can be used to replace tissue that has lost its function, as in the case of heart problems. They can also be used to treat genetic diseases by being implanted into the donor before the genetic disease has developed. This has led to some success when treating brain disease.

Some plant cells behave in a similar way to stem cells. They can continue to grow and specialise throughout their life, whereas animal cells lose this ability when they mature. This can be demonstrated by taking cuttings from plants. These cuttings or sections of the plant are capable, under the correct conditions, of growing into an identical plant.

Animal cells only divide to repair and replace once growth is reached: the only exception being stem cells, which retain the ability to divide, grow and then specialise.

QUICK TEST

1. How many daughter cells does mitosis produce?
2. How many chromosomes do the daughter cells have?
3. What is mitosis used for?
4. What are chromosomes made of?
5. Does asexual reproduction require one parent or two?
6. Does asexual reproduction produce variation in individuals?
7. What type of individuals does it produce?
8. What is a stem cell?
9. Where can we find stem cells?
10. How many bases does DNA have?

Meiosis and fertilisation

Meiosis is a type of cell division that occurs in the formation of gametes (sex cells) in the reproductive organs (testes and ovaries in humans). It produces cells that have half the number of chromosomes. These cells, which have 23 chromosomes, are called *haploid cells*. Fertilisation restores the normal number of chromosomes to 46 (*diploid cell*) – most body cells are diploid.

Meiosis

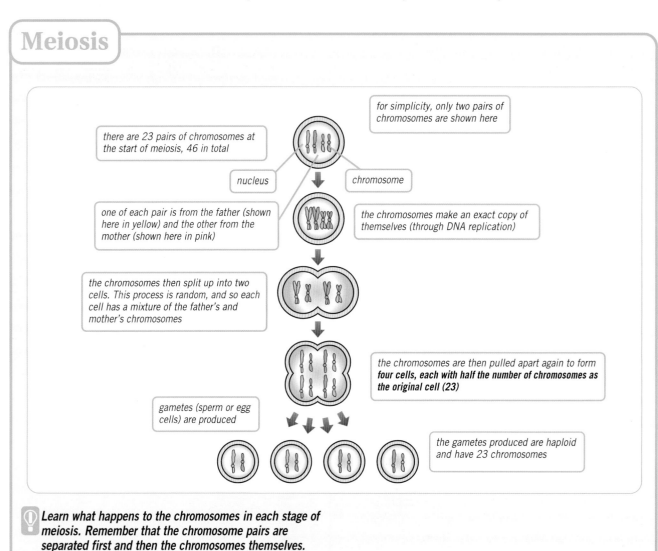

there are 23 pairs of chromosomes at the start of meiosis, 46 in total

for simplicity, only two pairs of chromosomes are shown here

nucleus

chromosome

one of each pair is from the father (shown here in yellow) and the other from the mother (shown here in pink)

the chromosomes make an exact copy of themselves (through DNA replication)

the chromosomes then split up into two cells. This process is random, and so each cell has a mixture of the father's and mother's chromosomes

the chromosomes are then pulled apart again to form **four cells, each with half the number of chromosomes as the original cell (23)**

gametes (sperm or egg cells) are produced

the gametes produced are haploid and have 23 chromosomes

Learn what happens to the chromosomes in each stage of meiosis. Remember that the chromosome pairs are separated first and then the chromosomes themselves.

Sexual reproduction and fertilisation 1

In fertilisation, the male gamete joins with a female gamete to produce a fertilised egg cell called a **zygote**. During fertilisation, the 23 single chromosomes in the sperm cell pair up with the 23 chromosomes in the egg cell. They pair up with their opposite number, that is, number four with number four and so on. Fertilisation restores the number of chromosomes to the **diploid number** of 46 or 23 pairs.

During the process of meiosis, it is a matter of chance which chromosomes make up the sperm and the egg. It is also a matter of chance which sperm fertilises which egg during fertilisation.

Meiosis and fertilisation give rise to variation in the individual, as the offspring will inherit a combination of the father's and mother's genes.

Any offspring will not be genetically identical because the process is random. Each sperm and egg contains different alleles.

Sexual reproduction and fertilisation 2

The process that determines which sperm will fertilise which egg is also random. Mutations may also occur during growth, leading to further variation.

Variation between individuals is partly due to the **inheritance** of genes from the parents. It is also a result of the **environment** in which the offspring lives and grows.

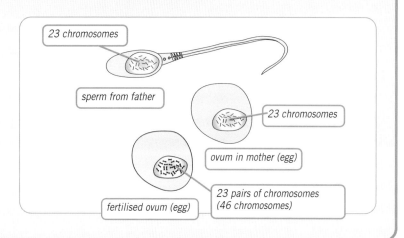

23 chromosomes

sperm from father

23 chromosomes

ovum in mother (egg)

fertilised ovum (egg)

23 pairs of chromosomes (46 chromosomes)

The inheritance of sex

When all the chromosomes are laid out in pairs, the **23rd** pair are **the sex chromosomes**. They determine whether you are a boy or a girl. All other chromosomes contain information about various characteristics. In a male, one of the sex chromosomes will be shorter than the other: this is the Y chromosome. Females have two X chromosomes that are the same size.

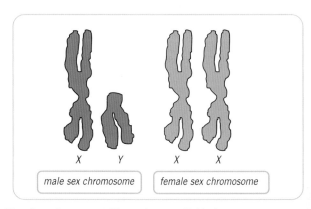

X   Y   X   X

male sex chromosome | female sex chromosome

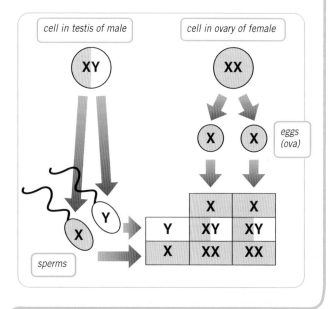

cell in testis of male | cell in ovary of female

XY

XX

X   X

eggs (ova)

sperms

X   Y

	X	X
Y	XY	XY
X	XX	XX

The female ovary will produce only X chromosomes during meiosis.

The male testis will produce half X chromosome sperms and half Y chromosome sperms. During fertilisation, the egg may join with either the X sperm or the Y sperm. We can show this information in a Punnett square diagram.

This diagram shows that each time a couple have children, there is a 50% chance that it will be a male and a 50% chance that it will be a female.

The 50% chance of having a boy or a girl is, however, only a probability. It is possible that all children could be girls.

> *The inheritance of sex is a common exam question. Make sure that you learn the Punnett square diagram.*

QUICK TEST

1. How many chromosomes are there in a haploid cell?
2. How many chromosomes are there in a diploid cell?
3. What is a zygote?
4. What is the probability of a couple's first child being a boy?
5. What is the probability of their second child being a girl?
6. If the 23rd pair of chromosomes are XY, will the offspring be male or female?
7. How many chromosomes would a cat's egg cell have, if the body cell of a cat has 38 chromosomes?
8. If a human baby inherits an X chromosome from its father, what sex would it be?

Genes, chromosomes and DNA

DNA is a chemical found in the nucleus of cells. It dictates the characteristics of organisms. Scientists may be able to cure diseases and solve crimes by studying DNA.

Inheritance

Inside nearly all cells is a nucleus. The nucleus **contains instructions** that control all your characteristics, called the **genetic code**. The instructions are carried on **chromosomes**. Genes, found on the chromosome, control each particular **characteristic**. Different genes control the development of different characteristics.

Inside human cells there are **46 chromosomes or 23 pairs** of chromosomes. Other animals have different numbers of chromosomes.

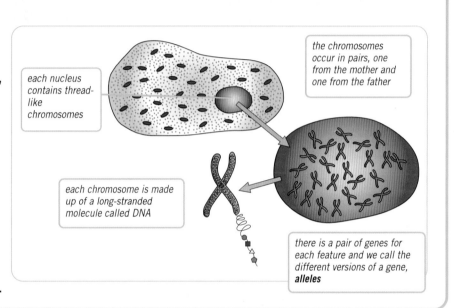

each nucleus contains thread-like chromosomes

the chromosomes occur in pairs, one from the mother and one from the father

each chromosome is made up of a long-stranded molecule called DNA

there is a pair of genes for each feature and we call the different versions of a gene, *alleles*

DNA molecule

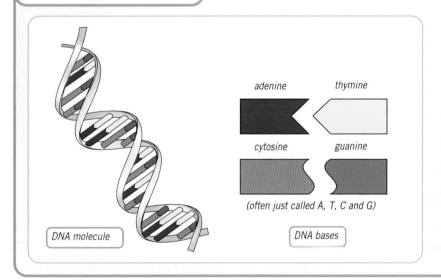

DNA molecule

adenine   thymine

cytosine   guanine

(often just called A, T, C and G)

DNA bases

The 'arms' of a chromosome are made up of a coiled up DNA molecule. A DNA molecule is joined together by chemical bases, like the rungs in a ladder. There are four bases: adenine (A), thymine (T), cytosine (C) and guanine (G). The base 'A' always pairs with 'T' and 'C' with 'G' to make up the rungs of the ladder.

The two sides of the ladder are coiled together to form a **double helix**.

DNA and protein synthesis 1

A gene is a length of DNA containing a small part of the genetic code. Proteins, made up of amino acids, control our characteristics and the growth and repair of cells. Genes control which protein a cell makes and so also control the development, structure and function of the whole organism. A process called **protein synthesis** explains just how genes code for a particular protein. Protein synthesis begins in the nucleus and ends in the cytoplasm of cells.

DNA and protein synthesis 2

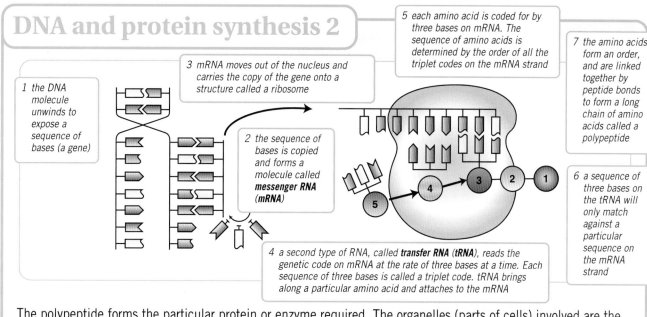

1 the DNA molecule unwinds to expose a sequence of bases (a gene)

2 the sequence of bases is copied and forms a molecule called **messenger RNA (mRNA)**

3 mRNA moves out of the nucleus and carries the copy of the gene onto a structure called a ribosome

4 a second type of RNA, called **transfer RNA (tRNA)**, reads the genetic code on mRNA at the rate of three bases at a time. Each sequence of three bases is called a triplet code. tRNA brings along a particular amino acid and attaches to the mRNA

5 each amino acid is coded for by three bases on mRNA. The sequence of amino acids is determined by the order of all the triplet codes on the mRNA strand

6 a sequence of three bases on the tRNA will only match against a particular sequence on the mRNA strand

7 the amino acids form an order, and are linked together by peptide bonds to form a long chain of amino acids called a polypeptide

The polypeptide forms the particular protein or enzyme required. The organelles (parts of cells) involved are the nucleus, where DNA is found, and the ribosomes, found in the cytoplasm of the cell.

Human Genome Project

The Human Genome Project was completed in 2003. It aimed to work out the sequence of bases in human chromosomes and to identify all the genes in human DNA and study them. The benefits included improved diagnosis of disease and earlier detection of genetic diseases, such as breast cancer and Alzheimer's, in families.

The use of DNA in forensic science was also greatly improved as a result of the project. It is now possible to identify suspects, clear the wrongly accused, identify paternity and match organ donors with recipients.

A person's 'DNA fingerprint' is unique. There is an extremely small chance of two people sharing the same fingerprint. Scientists can identify a region of DNA that is unique to one person and then build up a profile.

Embryo screening

The term 'designer baby' refers to the use of pre-implantation diagnosis of embryos (detecting disease or determining sex) using the IVF technique, where eggs are fertilised with sperm outside of the body. Healthy embryos are then implanted in the womb for growth.

In the UK, it is currently illegal to pre-determine the sex of a baby, unless it is linked in some way to a genetic disease. Some people may hope to have a baby with the genetic make-up to enable them to cure an existing child. This procedure is still under discussion and each case is dealt with and approved on a strictly case-by-case basis. Many people believe that this process interferes with nature and is not morally acceptable.

In the future, it may be possible to 'cure' diseases by replacing faulty sections of DNA. This practice is called germ line therapy. It may also be possible to create real designer babies, with specific features and levels of intelligence. Is this ethical?

1 Where is DNA found?

2 What are genes?

3 What are long chains of amino acids called?

4 How many bases code for one amino acid?

5 On which organelle does protein synthesis take place?

6 What is the name of the molecule formed when DNA is copied?

7 Where are genes found?

8 What is the process that makes proteins?

9 How many chromosomes does a human body cell have and where are they found?

10 What are proteins made up of?

Homeostasis

Homeostasis is the mechanism by which the body *maintains a constant internal environment*. The nervous system and hormones enable us to respond to external changes in the environment by monitoring and changing our *internal* environment. Hormonal effects tend to be *slower, long lasting* and *can affect a number of organs*. Nervous control is *much quicker* but its effects *don't last very* long. Nervous control is also *confined to a particular area* of the body.

Skin and body temperature

Humans are warm blooded and have mechanisms that keep our body temperature constant. Our body's reaction to changes in temperature is controlled by the thermoregulatory centre in the brain. This centre has receptors sensitive to the temperature of the blood flowing through the brain.

The skin also has receptors that send impulses to the centre in the brain giving information about skin temperature.

Inside your body the temperature always stays around the same temperature, 37°C. This is because the **enzymes** involved in the body's chemical reactions work best at this temperature.

When it is hot
- **Blood vessels** at the surface of the skin **widen**, allowing more blood to flow to the surface. This process is called **vasodilation**.

- You look flushed and heat is lost as it **radiates** from the skin.
- **Sweat glands** begin to secrete sweat. The sweat **evaporates** from the skin and takes away **heat energy**.
- **Panting** helps animals that do not sweat keep cool.

When it is cold
- **Blood vessels** at the surface of the skin **contract** so that very little blood gets to the surface. This process is called **vasoconstriction**.
- You look pale and very little heat is lost by radiation.
- **Sweat glands** stop producing sweat.
- Many warm-blooded animals also have a thick layer of fat beneath their skin that helps **insulate** the body in cold weather.
- You may **shiver**. This **quick contraction** of muscles produces extra heat to warm the body.
- Increased respiration also helps to generate heat, as does exercise.

Hormones and diabetes

Hormones are **chemical messengers** produced by glands known as **endocrine glands**. Hormones **travel in the** **blood plasma** to target organs. **Diabetes** is a disease caused by producing too little of the hormone insulin.

Diabetes

Diabetes results when the **pancreas does not make enough of the hormone insulin** and sometimes none at all. As a consequence, blood sugar levels rise and very little glucose is absorbed by the cells for respiration. This can make the sufferer tired and thirsty. If untreated, it leads to weight loss and even death.

Diabetes can be controlled in two ways: alteration to diet can be all that is needed to control some diabetes. In more severe cases where no insulin is produced, diabetics have to **inject themselves with insulin** before meals. This causes the liver to convert the glucose into glycogen straight away.

Pancreas and homeostasis

The **pancreas** is one of the organs involved in homeostasis: it **maintains the level of glucose (sugar) in the blood** so that there is enough for respiration. The pancreas secretes two hormones into the blood, **insulin and glucagon**.

If blood sugar levels are **too high**, which could be the case after a high carbohydrate meal, special cells in the pancreas detect these changes and release insulin. The **liver** responds to the amount of insulin in the

blood, takes up glucose and **stores it as glycogen. Blood sugar levels then return to normal.**

If blood sugar levels are **too low**, which could be the case during exercise, the pancreas secretes **glucagon**. **Glucagon** stimulates the **conversion of stored glycogen in the liver back into glucose** which is released into the blood. **Blood sugar levels return to normal.**

 Remember, insulin lowers blood sugar levels and glucagon raises blood sugar levels.

The kidneys

The kidneys are organs of **excretion**: they remove the waste products urea, excess water, and ions such as salt. First, they **filter** the blood and then **reabsorb** what the body needs. The kidney plays a major role in homeostasis by controlling the amount of water we have in our body, as well as the removal of excess substances and the poisonous substance urea. Excess water is removed in the kidneys and this makes up urine. It is also removed by sweating. The amount you sweat, and so lose water, obviously affects how much **urine** is produced. When it is hot, more water will be lost through sweating and so more water must be taken in to balance this loss. The control of water in the body is called **osmoregulation** and is monitored by the pituitary gland in the brain. How much water is reabsorbed depends on a hormone called **ADH** (antidiuretic hormone).

1. Why does sweating help keep us cool?
2. Can you explain why you look pale in cold weather?
3. What is homeostasis?
4. What two hormones does the pancreas produce?
5. What other organ is involved in controlling blood sugar levels?
6. What does the liver do with excess glucose?
7. What causes diabetes?
8. How can diabetes be treated?
9. What is the kidney's main role?
10. What is osmoregulation?

Farming

Food is vital to our existence. It is now produced in a number of ways to try to meet the needs of the rising human population. Genetic modification, selective breeding and intensive farming have enabled us to produce bigger, better, faster growing and higher yielding plants and animals.

Intensive farming of animals

Intensive farming aims to reduce energy losses in food chains and provide more food as a result.

Farmers can restrict the movement of animals, keep them warm and use antibiotics to hold disease at bay. As a result, they won't need feeding as much. This method will also produce much more food, as the animals grow quicker with less exercise. It also means less energy is lost at this stage of the food chain. There are also labour savings, meaning that the end produce will be cheaper to buy.

This method of farming also has disadvantages. Keeping animals confined is regarded by many as cruel. There is also some worry over the use of antibiotics. They are an added expense for the farmer and consumers worry that they may enter the food chain. Keeping the temperature constant would add to the cost of rearing animals. Examples of intensive farming include battery hens and fish farming.

Intensive farming of plants

Intensive farming attempts to produce more food from an area of land. It involves controlling weeds and pests, meaning that the plant's energy losses are reduced. Unfortunately, this also means that pesticides and fertilisers are needed.

Hydroponics is the growth of plants, without soil, in a special medium such as peat. This is useful in areas where the soil is infertile. Plants need support and carefully controlled mineral levels. They are grown in glasshouses, where the factors affecting growth and diseases can be controlled.

Intensive farming produces quality food, and more than enough of it to supply the needs of those in Europe. It also creates many problems. A possible solution to some of the problems is **organic farming**.

Organic farming

Organic farming produces less food per area of land and can be expensive because of the cost of labour and management. Organic food must be grown to comply with strict regulations. It attempts to leave the countryside as it is, and is kinder to animals.

Organic farming grows plants without the use of artificial fertilisers, herbicides and pesticides. This does mean that weeding becomes a labour-intensive task. It uses **manure and compost as a fertiliser, sets aside land** to allow wild plants and animals to flourish and relies upon **biological control of pests**.

The biological control of pests is the use of other animals that eat the pests to control them: for example, ladybirds to eat greenfly. It is not as effective as using pesticides and herbicides, but produces no harmful effects if carefully controlled.

Crops are rotated and seed plant times are varied to make full use of the land and prevent the plants from removing all nutrients from the soil.

Organic farmers often grow plants that are able to fix (capture) nitrogen from the atmosphere and turn it into the nutrient, nitrate. They do not harvest this crop. It is simply left and ploughed into the soil to improve fertility.

 Learn the arguments for and against intensive farming. Look at the benefits of its alternative, organic farming.

Greenhouses

Crop yields can be improved by growing plants in ideal, climate-controlled conditions, like greenhouses. A greenhouse allows the farmer or horticulturalist to control all the factors needed to **increase the rate of photosynthesis** and also prevents external factors, such as birds, from destroying the crop. The plants are not fully exposed to the natural elements.

Greenhouses work by trapping heat from the sun. The floor of the greenhouse heats up and heats the layer of air above it. This hot air rises up to the top of the greenhouse and is replaced by cooler air that, in turn, is also heated and rises. The warmer air at the top of the greenhouse is replaced and sinks back to the bottom, where it is heated up again.

The ground and air absorb sufficient heat during the day to keep the greenhouse relatively warm at night. Additional heating systems can be used because the amount of sunlight varies from day to day. Greenhouses often have some sort of plumbing system, to ensure that the soil stays moist and nutrients are distributed evenly.

One problem that does occur in a greenhouse is that of pests. They can be controlled by using pesticides or biological pest controls (predators specific to the pest). Unlike pesticides, a biological pest control leaves intact useful creatures such as ladybirds and bees.

Maximising food production – fish farming

problem is to use insecticides to kill the lice or to introduce another type of fish, called wrasse, to the nets. The wrasse will feed on the lice.

Salmon raised in this way do not look the same pinky colour as wild salmon, due to their diet being different. Artificial colours are added to the meat before it reaches the supermarkets so it looks like wild salmon. They also contain less of the good omega 3 oils.

Fish are now being farmed in response to the dangerously low levels of sea and river stocks we are currently experiencing as a result of over fishing.

In fish farms, fish are raised and bred in enclosed areas that are designed to be a large cage or net floating in a lake or the sea. Salmon and trout are commonly raised in this way. Artificially fertilised salmon eggs from aquarium tanks are released into the nets. They are fed a carefully controlled diet of food pellets, with any excess dropping out of the nets and on to the floor. The nets protect the salmon from predators, such as seagulls and seals, and also have the effect of **restricting the movement** of the large numbers of fish that they contain. This maximises the transfer of energy from the food, as no energy is used up in movement. As a result, the fish put on weight.

Fish reared in this manner, however, can suffer from parasites called fish lice. One way of dealing with this

QUICK TEST

1. What could be used as an alternative to fertilisers?
2. Why do you think organic products are more expensive than non-organic products?
3. What is 'hydroponics'?
4. How do nitrogen fixing plants help to improve the soil?
5. How do greenhouses keep warm?
6. How are pests controlled in a greenhouse?
7. Which animals feed on salmon fish lice?
8. Why aren't the salmon in a fish farm eaten by predators?

The environment

Humans continue to exploit the environment with our advancing technologies, growing population and our consumption of natural resources and production of vast amounts of waste.

Some animals and plants survive in extreme environments which are not influenced by human activity.

Human activity

Today, people are using more resources, and with more intensity, than at any point in human history. People around the world have different impacts on the environment, **depending on the economic and industrial conditions they are born into**. The **developed world** consumes more energy and produces more waste than the **developing world**. A child born today in an industrialised country will consume more energy and produce more pollution in his or her lifetime than 40 children born in developing countries.

In the developed world, education and family planning have helped to steady the population growth: in developing countries, population numbers continue to rise. As living standards rise in developing countries, more pressure is put on natural resources, such as fossil fuels and land. More and more land is either being built on, to house the rising population, or intensively farmed to produce food. Forests are

disappearing, species are under threat from hunting and over-fishing, and the pollution of land and water is increasing. The **growth of industrialisation**, such as manufacturing, mining, power generation and transport, has had a major impact on the environment, using up vast amounts of water and other non-renewable sources of energy. These industries also release harmful gases into the atmosphere.

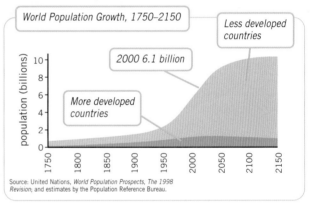

World Population Growth, 1750–2150

Less developed countries

2000 6.1 billion

More developed countries

population (billions)

Source: United Nations, *World Population Prospects, The 1998 Revision*; and estimates by the Population Reference Bureau.

Deforestation

Scientists know for certain that human activity is changing the atmosphere and leading, in particular, to a build up of carbon dioxide. Humans have been cutting down forests for 10,000 years. Forests are sustainable and replace themselves over the years or are replanted. However this is not being done.

The result is a reduction in forests known as **deforestation**. Deforestation reduces the number of photosynthesising organisms by destroying either the trees themselves or the vegetation in the habitat. As a result, the level of carbon dioxide in the atmosphere rises.

Clearing forests by burning further increases the level of carbon dioxide in the atmosphere: rising levels of carbon dioxide increase the greenhouse effect and lead to global warming.

Tropical rainforests are disappearing at an alarming rate. These forests produce around 40% of the world's oxygen and are home to an estimated 50% of all species on Earth. If these habitats are lost, they can never be replaced.

Conservation

We need to find a way to maintain some quality of life for future generations. This process is known as **sustainable development**.

It is important that we protect our food supply, maintain **biodiversity** and conserve resources, as we do not know what the future may hold. **Conservation** techniques include reforestation and replacement planting.

Replanting forests maintains biodiversity and prevents the build up of carbon dioxide. **Reforestation** can take place in the same area or in a different spot, but a new forest in a new area may not have the same biodiversity as the old one.

Another conservation technique is coppicing. **Coppicing**

is the art of cutting down trees to ground level in order to promote vigorous regrowth and provide a supply of timber for future use. Coppicing allows light back into the woodland and prompts the flowering of plants. It is usually done on a rotation basis so that each stage of regrowth can support a slightly different ecosystem. Coppicing actually prolongs the life of trees, by cutting back old wood and promoting new growth.

Extreme environments

The conditions in **extreme environments** determine which animals and plants exist and survive.

Deep sea volcanic vents were only discovered in 1977. They are regions on the ocean floor where fluids and gases from the Earth's crust, like methane and hydrogen sulphide, seep through. They occur along mid-ocean ridges.

These vents are found so far down in the ocean that there is no light for photosynthetic organisms to survive. So how does life exist?

Bacteria are the primary producers and begin the existing food webs. They use the hydrogen sulphide (that smells like rotten eggs) and oxygen to make energy, and then use the energy to make food for other organisms. They use chemicals to obtain energy, not light, in a process called chemosynthesis. Proteins in the bacteria are resistant to the heat and can withstand the extremely high temperatures (up to 400°C).

For reasons scientists cannot understand, the animals that survive in the vents are unusually large: an example is the tube worm that can be up to 1.5 metres long. These tube worms have no digestive system. They survive because the bacteria lining their insides provide

them with food. Other organisms found living in the vents are giant clams, crabs and shrimps.

Other examples of extreme environments that have promoted adaptation are the Antarctic and high altitudes. In the Antarctic, animals have had to adapt to the extreme cold. Instances of adaptation include whales, seals and birds that have an insulating layer of fat. Other animals have special chemicals in their blood that prevent them from freezing. Many animals, like penguins, have developed a compact body shape and thick skin in order to retain body heat. Some animals migrate in the colder months.

High altitude animals are able to survive the low oxygen levels by possessing more haemoglobin and red blood cells. Their haemoglobin is able to bind with what little oxygen there is much more easily than normal.

QUICK TEST

1. What is 'coppicing'?
2. What is 'reforestation'?
3. How can we reduce the effects of deforestation?
4. How have organisms adapted to the lack of sunlight in deep sea volcanic vents?
5. Which organisms are the primary producers in the deep sea volcanic vents?
6. Which chemical is used for chemosynthesis?

Practice questions

Use the questions to test your progress. Check your answers on page 124.

1. Why would a mammoth, found in frozen soil, not have decayed?

   ....

2. Write down the word equation for photosynthesis.

   ....

3. What three factors limit the rate of photosynthesis?

   ....

4. Label the diagram of a plant cell.

   a ....   d ....

   b ....   e ....

   c ....   f ....

5. Label this animal cell.

   a ....

   b ....

   c ....

6. Name three differences between a plant cell and an animal cell.

   ....

7. How many chromosomes does a human body cell have before it divides by mitosis?

   ....

8. Where does meiosis occur and what does it produce?

   ....

9. What is the process in which water moves from an area of high concentration to an area of low concentration?

   ....

10. What is the standard body temperature of humans?

    ....

11. What is diabetes?

    ....

12. How can diabetes be treated?

    ....

13. What is the function of a) insulin and b) glucagon?

    ....

14. What happens to your blood vessels when your body is hot?

....

15. What is the difference between genotype and phenotype?

....

16. How many chromosomes does a sperm cell have?

....

17. What role does the liver play in controlling blood sugar levels?

....

18. Where does aerobic respiration take place in a cell?

....

19. Which body cells are haploid?

....

20. What does diploid mean and which cells in the body are diploid?

....

21. What is the Hayflick Limit?

....

22. Where are natural plant hormones found?

....

23. Name the three types of bacteria in the nitrogen cycle.

....

24. What factors are needed to decay a dead animal or plant?

....

25. What is the name of the process where the chromosome number is doubled from 46 to 92?

....

26. How many chromosomes will a human body cell have after it has divided by mitosis?

....

27. Name two ways to maximise food production.

....

28. Why does a plant wilt from lack of water?

....

29. What does a pyramid of biomass illustrate?

....

30. Name two major differences between asexual and sexual reproduction?

....

Atomic structure

An atom consists of a central *nucleus* surrounded by shells of electrons. The nucleus is found at the centre of the atom and contains protons and neutrons.

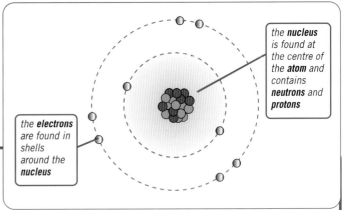

the **electrons** are found in shells around the **nucleus**

the **nucleus** is found at the centre of the **atom** and contains **neutrons** and **protons**

Elements

A substance that is made of **only one type of atom** is called an element. Elements cannot be broken down into simpler substances by chemical means. Atoms of different elements have different properties. About 100 different elements have been discovered. The elements can be represented by symbols. These symbols are often displayed in periodic tables.

💡 *Elements in the same group of the periodic table have similar properties because they have the same number of electrons in their outer shells.*

Structure of the atom

Atoms are made from three different types of particles:

protons

neutrons

electrons

Protons have a **mass of one atomic mass unit (amu)** and a **charge of 1+**.

Neutrons also have a **mass of one atomic mass unit** but **no charge**.

Electrons have a **negligible mass** and a **charge of 1−**.

In all neutral atoms there is no overall charge, and so the number of protons must be equal to the number of electrons.

Particle	Mass	Charge
Protons	1	+1
Neutrons	1	0
Electrons	negligible	−1

You may have seen two numbers written next to an element's symbol. These numbers are the mass number and the atomic number. They give us information about the particles inside the atom.

The **mass number** is the number of protons added to the number of neutrons. It is sometimes called the nucleon number.

The **atomic number** is the number of protons. All the atoms of a particular element (for example carbon) have the same number of protons. For example, carbon atoms always have six protons. This is sometimes called the proton number.

💡 *All atoms of the same element have the same number of protons and electrons.*

Sodium has an atomic number of 11, and so every sodium atom has 11 protons. A sodium atom has no overall charge, and so the number of electrons must be the same as the number of protons. Sodium atoms, therefore, have 11 electrons. The number of neutrons is given by the mass number minus the atomic number: for example, with sodium that is 23 − 11 = 12 neutrons.

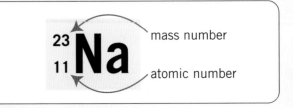

$^{23}_{11}$**Na** mass number / atomic number

💡 *Be familiar with the mass and charge of the three types of particle found inside an atom.*

Isotopes

Isotopes of an element have the **same number of protons** but a **different number of neutrons**. Isotopes, therefore, have the same atomic number but a different mass number.

Chlorine has two isotopes:

17 protons
17 electrons
18 neutrons

$^{35}_{17}Cl$

17 protons
17 electrons
20 neutrons

$^{37}_{17}Cl$

These isotopes have slightly different physical properties but will react identically in chemical reactions because they have identical numbers of electrons.

Electron structure

Electrons occupy the lowest available shell (or level). This is the shell closest to the nucleus. When it is full, the electrons start to fill the second shell, and so on. In our model, the first shell may contain up to two electrons while the second and third shells may contain up to eight electrons. The **electron structure of an atom is important because it determines how the atom will react**.

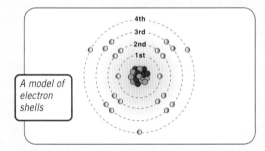

A model of electron shells

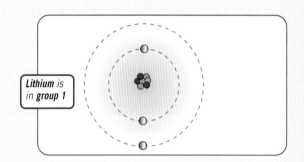

Lithium is in group 1

Magnesium

number of protons = 12
number of electrons = 12
electron structure = 2, 8, 2

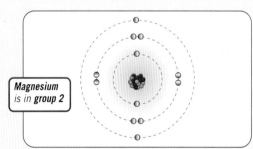

Magnesium is in group 2

Lithium

number of protons = 3
number of electrons = 3
electron structure = 2, 1

Lithium is in group 1 of the periodic table because it has one electron in its outer shell. It is in period 2 of the periodic table because it has two shells of electrons.

Magnesium is in group 2 of the periodic table because it has two electrons in its outer shell. It is in period 3 of the periodic table because it has three shells of electrons.

QUICK TEST

1. What does the nucleus contain?
2. Which particles are found in shells around the nucleus?
3. What is the charge and mass of a proton?
4. What is the charge and mass of an electron?
5. What is the charge and mass of a neutron?
6. What is the mass number of an element?
7. What is the atomic number of an element?
8. How are isotopes of an element the same?
9. How are isotopes of an element different?
10. Why do isotopes of an element react in the same way?

Balancing equations

Symbol equations show the type and ratio of the atoms involved in a reaction. The *reactants* are placed on the left-hand side of the equation. The *products* are placed on the right-hand side of the equation. *There must always be the same number of each type of atom on both sides of the equation.* This is because atoms are never made or destroyed during chemical reactions.

Balancing the equation

Hydrogen burns in air to produce water vapour. This can be shown using a word equation:

hydrogen + oxygen → water

The word equation is useful, but it doesn't tell us **the ratio of hydrogen and oxygen molecules involved**. Balanced symbol equations show us this extra information.

First, replace the words with symbols. Hydrogen and oxygen both exist as molecules.

$H_2 + O_2 \rightarrow H_2O$

The formulas are all correct, but the equation isn't quite right. It doesn't **balance** because there are different numbers of atoms on each side of the equation. The formulas cannot be changed, but numbers can be added in front of the formulas to balance the equation.

Looking at the equation, we can see that there are two oxygen atoms on the left-hand side of the equation but only one oxygen atom on the right-hand side. A **2**, therefore, must be placed in front of the H_2O:

$H_2 + O_2 \rightarrow 2H_2O$

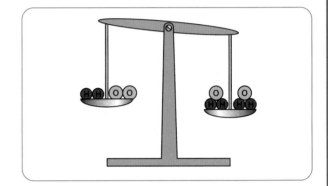

The oxygen atoms are now balanced: there are the same numbers of oxygen atoms on both sides of the equation. The hydrogen atoms, however, are no longer balanced. There are two hydrogen atoms on the left-hand side and four hydrogen atoms on the right-hand side. A **2** is then placed in front of the H_2:

$2H_2 + O_2 \rightarrow 2H_2O$

The equation is now balanced.

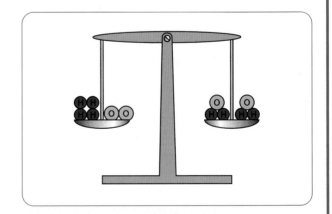

Balancing equations just needs a little practice. Deal with each type of atom in turn until everything balances.

State symbols

State symbols can be added to an equation to show extra information. They show what **state the reactants and products** are in.

The symbols are:

(s) for solid

(l) for liquid

(g) for gases

(aq) for aqueous or dissolved in water.

Example

Magnesium metal can be burnt in air to produce magnesium oxide. Magnesium and magnesium oxide are both solids. The part of the air that reacts when things are burnt is oxygen, which is a gas.

> magnesium + oxygen → magnesium oxide
>
> $2Mg_{(s)}$ + $O_{2(g)}$ → $2MgO_{(s)}$

! *When balancing equations, always check that the formulas that you have written down are correct.*

Precipitation reactions

Sometimes two solutions can react together to form a product which is insoluble. The insoluble product is called a precipitate. Hard water contains calcium or magnesium ions. These ions react with soap to make scum instead of lots of nice bubbles which we call a lather. This makes it difficult or 'hard' to clean things.

We can remove the calcium ions from hard water by adding sodium carbonate or 'washing soda'. The washing soda crystals dissolve in water to form a solution. The sodium carbonate solution reacts with the hard water which contains dissolved calcium sulphate to form calcium carbonate and sodium sulphate. The calcium carbonate is insoluble so it forms a precipitate. The water has been softened because the calcium ions have been removed.

> sodium carbonate + calcium sulphate → calcium carbonate + sodium sulphate
>
> $Na_2CO_{3(aq)}$ $CaSO_{4(aq)}$ $CaCO_{3(s)}$ $Na_2SO_{4(aq)}$

1 How many different types of atom are present in $CaCO_3$?

2 What is the name of the element with the symbol Ca?

3 A carbon monoxide molecule has the formula CO. Write down the type and number of atoms in one molecule of carbon monoxide.

4 A carbon dioxide molecule has the formula CO_2. Write down the type and number of atoms in one molecule of carbon dioxide.

5 A sulphur dioxide molecule has the formula SO_2. Write down the type and number of atoms in one molecule of sulphur dioxide.

6 Why must there be the same number of each type of atom on both sides of an equation?

7 Balance the equation, $Na + Cl_2 \longrightarrow NaCl$

8 Balance the equation, $H_2 + Cl_2 \longrightarrow HCl$

9 Balance the equation, $C + CO_2 \longrightarrow CO$

10 What does the state symbol (l) indicate?

Ionic and covalent bonding

Ionic bonding involves the *transfer of electrons*. This forms *ions* with opposite charges, which then *attract each other*. Covalent bonding involves the *sharing* of electrons. The shared pairs of electrons hold the atoms together.

Ionic bonding

All atoms wish to get a full outer shell of electrons, like the noble gas elements. **Ionic** bonding involves the transfer of electrons from one atom to another. Metal atoms in groups 1 and 2, such as sodium or calcium, lose electrons to get a full outer shell of electrons. Overall, they become **positively charged** (electrons have a negative charge).

Non-metal atoms in group 6 and 7, such as oxygen or chlorine, gain electrons to obtain a full outer shell, and so they become **negatively charged**. An ion is an atom or a group of atoms with a charge. An atom or group of atoms becomes an ion by gaining or losing electrons.

> When drawing dot and cross diagrams to show ionic or covalent bonding, just draw the outer shell of electrons.

> In the dot and cross diagrams, the electrons drawn as dots and the electrons drawn as crosses are identical. We draw them like this so it easier to see what happens when the electrons move.

Sodium chloride

Sodium reacts with chlorine to make sodium chloride.

sodium + chlorine → sodium chloride

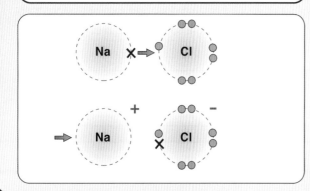

- The sodium atom transfers one electron from its outer shell to the chlorine atom.
- Both the sodium and chlorine atoms have a full outer shell.
- The sodium atom has lost an electron so has a 1+ charge. It is now a **sodium ion**.
- The chlorine atom has gained an electron and so has a 1– charge. It is now a **chloride ion**.
- **The attraction between these two oppositely charged ions is called an ionic bond and holds the compound together.**

> Compounds are made when atoms of two or more elements are chemically combined.

Magnesium oxide

Magnesium reacts with oxygen to make magnesium oxide.

magnesium + oxygen → magnesium oxide

- The magnesium atom transfers two electrons from its outer shell to the oxygen atom.
- Both the magnesium and oxygen atom now have a full outer shell.
- The magnesium atom has lost two electrons and so has a 2+ charge. It is now a **magnesium ion**.
- The oxygen atom has gained two electrons and so has

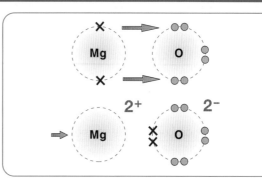

a 2– charge. It is now an **oxide ion**.
- The attraction between these two oppositely charged ions is called an ionic bond and holds the compound together.

Covalent bonding

Covalent bonding occurs between atoms of non-metal elements. The atoms **share pairs of electrons** so that all the atoms gain a full outer shell of electrons.

Hydrogen, H$_2$

Both the hydrogen atoms have just one electron. By sharing these electrons to form a single covalent bond, both atoms can get a full outer shell.

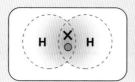

Hydrogen chloride, HCl

The hydrogen atom and the chlorine atom both need one more electron. They share a pair of electrons to form a single covalent bond and so they now both have a full outer shell.

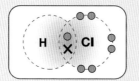

Methane, CH$_4$

The carbon atom has four electrons in its outer shell and so needs four more electrons to have a full shell. The carbon shares one pair of electrons with four different hydrogen atoms to form four single covalent bonds. Now, all the atoms have a full outer shell.

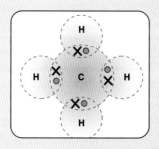

Ammonia, NH$_3$

The nitrogen atom has five outer electrons and so needs three more electrons for a full shell. It gains these electrons by sharing a pair of electrons with three hydrogen atoms, to form three single covalent bonds.

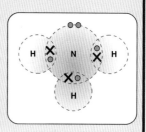

Water, H$_2$O

The oxygen atom has six outer electrons so needs two more electrons to get a full shell. The oxygen shares one pair of electrons with two hydrogen atoms, to form two single covalent bonds.

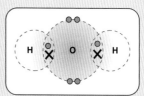

Oxygen, O$_2$

Both oxygen atoms have six outer electrons and so they need a share of two more electrons. They gain these by sharing two pairs of electrons to form a double covalent bond.

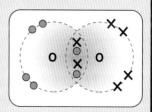

This section is very important. Make sure you know it really well.

QUICK TEST

1. How many outer electrons do elements in group 1 have?
2. How many outer electrons do elements in group 6 have?
3. If an element in group 1 loses an electron, what charge does it have?
4. If an element in group 6 gains two electrons, what charge does it have?
5. Draw a dot and cross diagram to show sodium reacting with chlorine.
6. What is an ionic bond?
7. What type of bonding occurs between non-metal atoms?
8. Draw a dot and cross diagram to show hydrogen reacting with chlorine.
9. Draw a dot and cross diagram to show the bonding in methane.

Ionic and covalent structures

Ionic bonding occurs between metal and non-metal atoms. It involves the transfer of electrons and the formation of ions. Covalent bonding occurs between non-metal atoms. It involves the sharing of electrons.

Ionic compounds

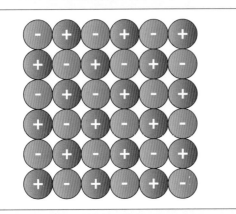

Ionic compounds are held together by the strong forces of attraction between **oppositely charged ions**. Ionic compounds have a regular structure. The strong forces of attraction between oppositely charged ions means that ionic compounds have **high melting and boiling points**. When dissolved in water, ionic compounds form solutions in which the **ions can move**. This means that these solutions can conduct electricity. Similarly, if ionic compounds are heated up so that they melt, the ions can move. Molten ionic compounds can also conduct electricity.

Simple covalent structures

Examples of simple covalent structures include:
■ chlorine molecules
■ oxygen molecules
■ hydrogen iodide molecules
■ methane molecules
■ water molecules.

These molecules are all formed **from small numbers of atoms**. There are very strong covalent bonds between the atoms in each molecule, but very weak forces of attraction between these molecules. As a consequence, molecular compounds have low melting and boiling points. Most are gases or liquids at room temperature.

Simple molecular compounds **do not conduct electricity** because they do not contain ions. They tend to be **insoluble in water**, although they may dissolve in other solvents.

Giant covalent substances

Examples of giant covalent (macromolecular) structures include:
■ diamond
■ graphite
■ silicon dioxide.

These structures are formed from a **large number of atoms**. The atoms in these structures are held together by **strong covalent bonds**. This means that these substances have **high melting and boiling points**. They are solids at room temperature. Like simple covalent molecules, giant covalent substances do not conduct electricity (except graphite) as they do not contain ions. They are also **insoluble in water**.

Diamond

Diamond is a form of the element **carbon**. Like other gemstones, it is prized for its rareness and its pleasing appearance. Diamond is also very hard. High quality diamonds are used to make jewellery. Other diamonds are used in industry for a variety of applications. The hardness and high melting point of diamond makes it an excellent cutting tool. Its special properties are caused by structure. Diamond is an example of a giant covalent substance. Each carbon atom is bonded to **four other carbon atoms by strong covalent bonds**.

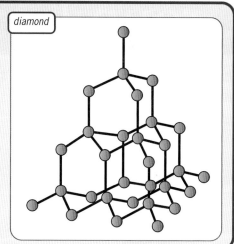

diamond

Graphite

Graphite is another form of the element carbon. In graphite, each carbon atom forms strong covalent bonds with three other carbon atoms in the same layer. The **bonding between layers**, however, **is much weaker**. This means that the layers can pass over each other quite easily, which is why graphite feels greasy.

If a potential difference is applied across graphite, the electrons in the weak bonds between layers move and so conduct electricity. Carbon in the form of graphite is the only non-metal element that conducts electricity.

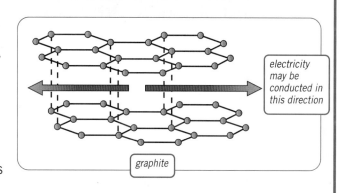

electricity may be conducted in this direction

graphite

Nanoparticles

Nano-science is the study of extremely small pieces of material. These tiny pieces are called nanoparticles. Scientists are currently researching the properties of new nanoparticles. These substances contain **just a few hundred atoms** and vary in size from 1 nm to 100 nm (a human hair has a width of about one hundred thousand nanometres). These materials have unique properties due to the very precise way in which the atoms are arranged. Scientists have found that many materials behave differently on such a small scale.

QUICK TEST

1. What type of structure do all ionic compounds form?

2. Why do ionic compounds have high melting and boiling points?

3. Why can ionic compounds conduct electricity when dissolved, but not when solid?

4. Why can ionic compounds conduct electricity when molten?

5. Give an example of a simple molecular compound.

6. Describe the bonding between atoms and between molecules in simple covalent molecular compounds.

7. Do simple molecular compounds conduct electricity?

8. Give two forms of carbon.

9. Why do giant covalent structures have very high melting points?

10. Why can graphite conduct electricity?

Group 1 – the alkali metals

The Group 1 metals are found on the far left-hand side of the periodic table.

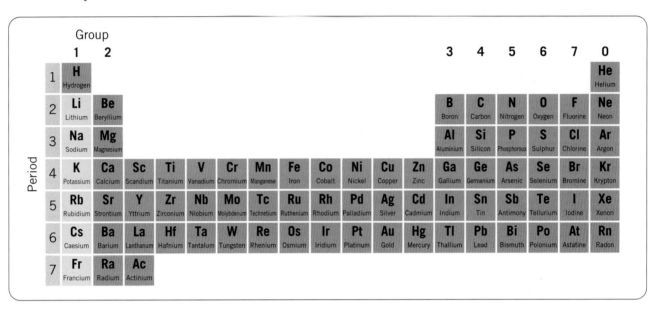

Reactions of the Group 1 metals with water

The metals lithium, sodium and potassium are all **less dense than water**. If these metals are placed in water they will float. All Group 1 metals react with water to produce hydrogen gas and an alkaline solution of a metal hydroxide.

Lithium

Lithium reacts with water to produce a solution of lithium hydroxide and hydrogen gas. We can test for the presence of hydrogen gas by placing a lighted splint nearby. If

lithium

hydrogen is present it will burn with a squeaky pop.

lithium + water $\rightarrow$ lithium hydroxide + hydrogen
$$2Li + 2H_2O \rightarrow 2LiOH + H_2$$

Sodium

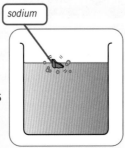

sodium

Sodium reacts more vigorously with water to produce a solution of sodium hydroxide and hydrogen gas. The sodium moves around on the surface of the water as it reacts. If **universal**

indicator is added to the solution of sodium hydroxide that is made during this reaction, it will turn **purple**.

sodium + water $\rightarrow$ sodium hydroxide + hydrogen
$$2Na + 2H_2O \rightarrow 2NaOH + H_2$$

Potassium

Potassium is the most reactive of the three metals. The reaction between potassium and water is so **vigorous** that the hydrogen gas produced may ignite and burn with a lilac flame.

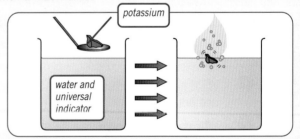

potassium

water and universal indicator

potassium + water $\rightarrow$ potassium hydroxide + hydrogen
$$2K + 2H_2O \rightarrow 2KOH + H_2$$

From these descriptions we can see that chemical reactions occur at different rates.

💡 *Alkali metals are so reactive that they must be stored under oil to stop them reacting with moisture or oxygen in the air.*

Why do all Group 1 metals react in a similar way?

The alkali metals are **all very reactive**. They have just one electron in their outer shell. Group 1 metals all have similar properties because they have similar electron structures. Alkali metals **react with non-metals to form ionic compounds**. For example, sodium reacts with chlorine to form sodium chloride.

sodium + chlorine → sodium chloride
$$2Na + Cl_2 \rightarrow 2NaCl$$

When they react, an alkali metal atom loses its outer electron to form ions with a 1+ charge.

$$Na \rightarrow Na^+ + e^-$$

The alkali metal atom has lost an electron so it is oxidised.

Group 1 metals form white compounds, which dissolve to form colourless solutions.

Why does potassium react more vigorously than lithium?

Reactivity increases as we go down the group, because the outer electron is further away from the nucleus and **it is easier for atoms to lose their outer electron**. There are **more shells shielding** the outer electron from the nucleus as we go down the group, and so it is easier for atoms to lose their outer electron.

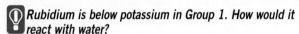 *Rubidium is below potassium in Group 1. How would it react with water?*

Why do melting and boiling points decrease down the group?

Melting and boiling points **decrease down the group**. Alkali metals are held together by metallic bonding. Metallic bonding is the attraction between the positive metal ions and the 'sea' of negative electrons. Down the group, the atoms get larger and this means that the strength of the **metallic bonding decreases**. It takes less energy to overcome the forces of attraction because these forces become weaker down the group. As a result, the alkali metals melt and boil at lower temperatures.

❶ Name the first three metals in Group 1.

❷ How many electrons are present in the outer shell of all Group 1 metals?

❸ Why do all the Group 1 metals have similar properties?

❹ What type of compounds do Group 1 metals form?

❺ What charge do Group 1 ions have?

❻ What is the trend in reactivity down Group 1 of the periodic table?

❼ Why does sodium float on water?

❽ What is the test for hydrogen gas?

❾ Give the symbol equation for the reaction between sodium and water.

❿ Give the symbol equation for the reaction between sodium and chlorine.

Group 7 – the halogens

The group 7 atoms are found on the right-hand side of the periodic table, next to the noble gases.

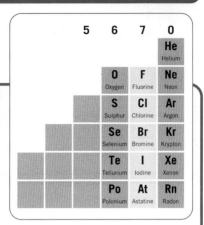

Characteristics of the halogen family

The halogen family includes fluorine, chlorine, bromine and iodine.

Fluorine

Fluorine is a very poisonous gas. Fluorine is a diatomic molecule with the formula F_2. It has a pale yellow colour.

Chlorine

Chlorine is a poisonous gas which should only be used in the fume cupboard. Chlorine is a diatomic molecule with the formula Cl_2. It has a pale green colour and is used in water purification and in the manufacture of pesticides and plastics.

Bromine

Bromine is a poisonous, dense liquid. It has a brown colour. Bromine is a diatomic molecule with the formula Br_2.

Iodine

Iodine exists as a dark grey, crystalline solid and, as a solid, is brittle and crumbly. Solid iodine is a poor electrical and thermal conductor. When warmed, iodine forms a purple vapour. Iodine solution can be used as an antiseptic and **to test for the presence of starch**. When iodine solution is placed on a material that contains starch, it turns blue/black. Iodine is diatomic, the formula is I_2.

💡 *Halogens have coloured vapours. Down the group, the colour of the vapour gets darker.*

Why do halogens react in a similar way?

Halogens have seven electrons in their outer shell. **Group 7 elements have similar properties because they have similar electron structures.** Halogens react with metal atoms to form **ionic compounds**. For example, chlorine reacts with calcium to form calcium chloride.

> chlorine + calcium → calcium chloride
> $$Ca \;+\; Cl_2 \;\rightarrow\; CaCl_2$$

When they react, a halogen atom gains an electron to form an ion with a 1– charge.

> $$Cl + e^- \rightarrow Cl^-$$

The halogen atom has gained an electron and so it is reduced.

Why do melting and boiling points increase down the group?

Melting and boiling points **increase down the group**. Group 7 atoms form molecules in which two atoms are joined together. Down the group, the atoms get larger and have more electrons. This means that the strength of attraction between **molecules** increases. It takes more energy to overcome these forces of attraction between molecules because the forces get stronger down the group. As a result, the halogens melt and boil at higher temperatures.

Why does fluorine react more vigorously than bromine?

Reactivity decreases down the group. When an atom reacts to form an ion, the new electron is being placed in a **shell further away from the nucleus**. As a result, it is harder for atoms to gain an electron further down the group. As we go down the group, there are **more shells of electrons shielding the new electron from the nucleus**. Once again, it is harder for atoms to gain a new electron further down the group.

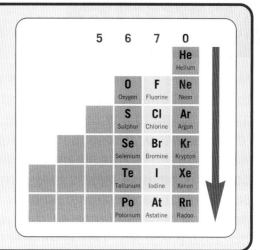

Displacement reactions involving halogens

We have seen how reactivity decreases down group 7. The most reactive halogen is fluorine, followed by chlorine, then bromine then iodine. **A more reactive halogen will displace a less reactive halogen from its solution.** Hence chlorine could displace bromine or iodine. However, while bromine could displace iodine it could not displace chlorine.

Example

Chlorine will displace iodine from a solution of potassium iodide.

potassium   potassium
iodide + chlorine → chloride + iodine
$$2KI + Cl_2 \rightarrow 2KCl + I_2$$

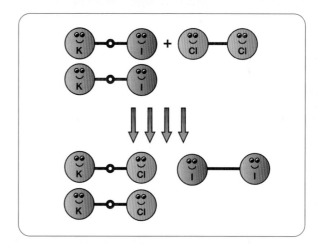

Elements in group 7 have similar properties and react with metals to form compounds in which the group 7 ion carries a 1− charge.

QUICK TEST

1. What is the name used for group 7?
2. What is the trend in the size of the atoms down group 7?
3. What is the trend in reactivity down group 7?
4. What safety precautions should be used when handling chlorine?
5. What is the trend in melting and boiling points down group 7?
6. What is the state of the first four halogens at room temperature?
7. What is the trend in the colour of the elements down group 7?
8. How is chlorine used?
9. What is iodine solution used for?
10. What would happen if chlorine gas was reacted with potassium bromide?

Metals

Metals have a *giant structure*. The electrons in the highest energy shells (the outer electrons) are not bound to any one atom, but are '*delocalised*' or free to move through the whole structure. This means that metals consist of positive metals *ions* surrounded by a sea of negative *electrons. Metallic bonding is the attraction between these positive ions and the negative electrons. This is an electrostatic attraction.*

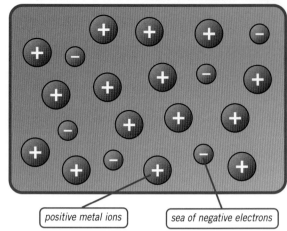

positive metal ions   sea of negative electrons

Properties of metals

Metallic bonding means that metals have several, very useful properties.

- The free electrons make metals **good electrical conductors**.
- The free electrons also make metals **good thermal conductors**.
- The strong attraction between the metal ions and the electrons means that metals can be drawn into **wires** as the ions slide over each other. Metals can also be **hammered into shape**.

The transition metals are found in the middle section of the periodic table. Copper, iron and nickel are examples of very useful transition metals. All transition metals have characteristic properties. They have:

- **high melting points** (except for mercury which is a liquid at room temperature)
- **high density**
- coloured compounds: for example, copper compounds are blue, iron (II) compounds are green and iron (III) compounds are a 'foxy' red.

They are also strong, tough and hard-wearing.

Transition metals are also much less reactive than group 1 metals. They all react much less vigorously with oxygen and water.

Many transition metals can **form ions with different charges**. This makes transition metals useful **catalysts** in many reactions.

Group													3	4	5	6	7	0
	1	**2**																
1	**H** Hydrogen																	**He** Helium
2	**Li** Lithium	**Be** Beryllium											**B** Boron	**C** Carbon	**N** Nitrogen	**O** Oxygen	**F** Fluorine	**Ne** Neon
3	**Na** Sodium	**Mg** Magnesium											**Al** Aluminium	**Si** Silicon	**P** Phosphorous	**S** Sulphur	**Cl** Chlorine	**Ar** Argon
4	**K** Potassium	**Ca** Calcium	**Sc** Scandium	**Ti** Titanium	**V** Vanadium	**Cr** Chromium	**Mn** Manganese	**Fe** Iron	**Co** Cobalt	**Ni** Nickel	**Cu** Copper	**Zn** Zinc	**Ga** Gallium	**Ge** Germanium	**As** Arsenic	**Se** Selenium	**Br** Bromine	**Kr** Krypton
5	**Rb** Rubidium	**Sr** Strontium	**Y** Yttrium	**Zr** Zirconium	**Nb** Niobium	**Mo** Molybdenum	**Tc** Technetium	**Ru** Ruthenium	**Rh** Rhodium	**Pd** Palladium	**Ag** Silver	**Cd** Cadmium	**In** Indium	**Sn** Tin	**Sb** Antimony	**Te** Tellurium	**I** Iodine	**Xe** Xenon
6	**Cs** Caesium	**Ba** Barium	**La** Lanthanum	**Hf** Hafnium	**Ta** Tantalum	**W** Tungsten	**Re** Rhenium	**Os** Osmium	**Ir** Iridium	**Pt** Platinum	**Au** Gold	**Hg** Mercury	**Tl** Thallium	**Pb** Lead	**Bi** Bismuth	**Po** Polonium	**At** Astatine	**Rn** Radon
7	**Fr** Francium	**Ra** Radium	**Ac** Actinium															

Period

- Metals
- Transition metals
- Non metals

Copper

Copper is a good electrical and thermal conductor. It can easily be bent into new shapes and does not corrode. Copper is widely used in electrical wiring and is also used to make water pipes.

Metal alloys

Alloys are made by mixing metals together.
Occasionally, alloys can even be made by mixing metals with non-metals. For example, to make steel, iron is mixed with carbon.

Nickel

Nickel is hard, shiny and dense. It is widely used to make coins. Nickel is also used as a catalyst in the manufacture of margarine.

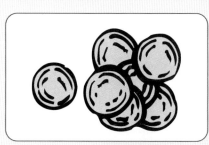

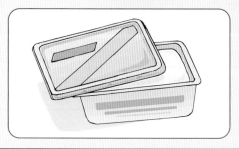

Iron

Iron made in the blast furnace is strong yet brittle. It is often made into steel. Steel is strong and cheap and is used in vast quantities. It is also heavy, however, and may rust. Iron and steel are useful structural materials. These metals are used to make buildings, bridges, ships, cars and trains. Iron is also used as a catalyst in the Haber process.

METALS

Chemistry

QUICK TEST

1. Why are metals able to conduct heat and electricity?
2. In which part of the periodic table are the transition metals found?
3. What are the characteristics of transition metals?
4. Why is copper used for electrical wiring?
5. Why is copper used for water pipes?
6. Why is iron made into steel?
7. Which items can be made from steel?
8. In which process is iron used as a catalyst?
9. Which items can be made from nickel?
10. Nickel is used as a catalyst for the manufacture of which foodstuff?

Relative formula mass

Relative atomic mass

The **relative atomic mass** (RAM) is used to compare the masses of different atoms. The relative atomic mass of an element is the average mass of its **isotopes** compared with an atom of carbon-12.

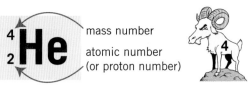

$^4_2$He — mass number / atomic number (or proton number)

RAM number of helium = 4

$^{24}_{12}$**Mg**

RAM number of magnesium = 24

Relative formula mass

The **relative formula mass** of a substance is worked out by adding together the relative atomic masses of all the atoms in the ratio indicated by the formula.

For carbon dioxide, CO_2:
The relative formula mass of CO_2 is 44.

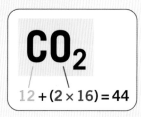

CO₂

$12 + (2 \times 16) = 44$

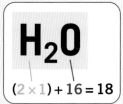

H₂O

$(2 \times 1) + 16 = 18$

For water, H_2O:
The relative formula mass of H_2O is 18.

The relative formula mass of a substance in grams is known as one mole of the substance. So one mole of CO_2 is 44 g and one mole of H_2O is 18 g.

For calcium hydroxide, $Ca(OH)_2$:

Calcium hydroxide is a solid made when water is added to calcium oxide.

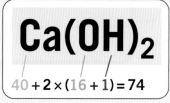

Ca(OH)₂

$40 + 2 \times (16 + 1) = 74$

A solution of calcium hydroxide is called limewater.

The number of moles of a substance present can be calculated using the formula:

$$\text{number of moles} = \frac{\text{mass of sample}}{\text{relative formula mass of the substance}}$$

Example
How many moles are there in 9 g of water?
The relative formula mass of water is 18.

$$\text{number of moles} = \frac{9}{18} = 0.5$$

There are 0.5 moles in 9 g of water.

Example
How many moles are there in 111 g of calcium hydroxide, $Ca(OH)_2$?
The relative formula mass of calcium hydroxide is 74.

$$\text{number of moles} = \frac{111}{74} = 1.5$$

There are 1.5 moles in 111 g.

Finding the empirical formula

The empirical formula is the simplest ratio of atoms in a formula.

Example

Find the **empirical formula** of **magnesium oxide** formed when 12 g of magnesium reacts with 8 g of oxygen atoms.

Deal with the magnesium and the oxygen separately.

	Mg	O
State the number of grams that combine.	12	8
Change the grams to moles (divide by A_r).	12/24	8/16
This is the ratio in which the atoms combine.	0.5	0.5
Get the ratio into its simplest form.	1	1

The simplest ratio of Mg : O is 1 : 1, so the formula is MgO.

Calculating the percentage composition of an element in a compound

Compounds consist of two or more different elements.

Percentage mass of an element in a compound

$$= \frac{\text{relative atomic mass} \times \text{no. of atoms}}{\text{relative formula mass}} \times 100\%$$

Example

Ammonium nitrate, NH_4NO_3, is used as a fertiliser.

Find the **percentage composition** of nitrogen in this compound.
- RAM of N = 14
- RAM of H = 1
- RAM of O = 16

The formula mass of NH_4NO_3 is:
- $14 + (4 \times 1) + 14 + (3 \times 16) = 80$

Percentage of nitrogen $= \dfrac{14 \times 2}{80} \times 100\% = 35\%$

- Ammonium nitrate is 35% nitrogen.

It is tempting to just skate over these difficult areas but you do need to practise them.

1. Give the relative atomic mass of sodium, Na.
2. Work out the relative formula mass of a nitrogen molecule, N_2.
3. Work out the relative formula mass of an oxygen molecule, O_2.
4. Work out the relative formula mass of magnesium oxide, MgO.
5. Work out the relative formula mass of a sulphur dioxide molecule, SO_2.
6. Calculate the percentage of hydrogen in NH_4NO_3.
7. Calculate the percentage of oxygen in NH_4NO_3.
8. Calculate the percentage of oxygen in magnesium oxide, MgO.
9. Calculate the percentage of magnesium in magnesium oxide, MgO.
10. Calculate the percentage of oxygen in sulphur dioxide, SO_2.

Calculating masses

The masses of *products* and *reactants* can be worked out using the balanced *equation* for the reaction.

Calculating the mass of products

What mass of water is produced when 8 g of hydrogen is burnt?

> Relative atomic mass
> H = 1
> O = 16

First, we can write down what happens during the reaction as a **word equation**.

> hydrogen + oxygen → water

Then, we can write it as a **balanced symbol equation**.

> $2H_2 + O_2 \rightarrow 2H_2O$

Next, we can calculate the **relative formula mass** of a hydrogen molecule and a water molecule.

The relative formula mass of hydrogen, H_2:

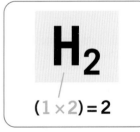

$(1 \times 2) = 2$

The relative formula mass of water, H_2O:

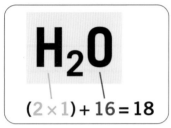

$(2 \times 1) + 16 = 18$

Now we can calculate the number of moles in 8 g of hydrogen.

> $$\text{number of moles} = \frac{\text{mass of sample}}{\text{RFM of the substance}}$$
> $$= \frac{8}{2} = 4 \text{ moles}$$

Next we must examine the balanced symbol equation. Every 2 moles of hydrogen make 2 moles of water. This means that if we start with 4 moles of hydrogen, we will finish up with 4 **moles** of water. Now, all we need to do is work out the mass of 4 moles of water. We can do this by rearranging our moles equation.

number of moles	×	RFM of the substance	=	mass of the sample
4	×	18	=	72

This shows that if 8 g of hydrogen is burnt completely, we will make 72 g of water vapour.

Calculating the mass of reactants 1

The equation for a reaction can also be used to calculate how much reactant should be used to produce a given amount of the product.

What mass of magnesium should be used to produce 60 g of magnesium oxide?

> Relative atomic mass
> Mg = 24
> O = 16

First, we can write down what happens during the reaction as a **word equation**.

> magnesium + oxygen → magnesium oxide

Then, we can write it as a **balanced symbol equation**.

> $2Mg + O_2 \rightarrow 2MgO$

Next, we can calculate the relative formula mass of magnesium oxide.

Calculating the mass of reactants 2

The relative formula mass of magnesium oxide, MgO:

The relative atomic mass of magnesium is given in the question as 24.

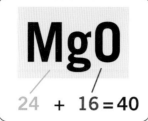

$24 + 16 = 40$

Now, we can calculate the number of moles in 60 g of magnesium oxide.

$$\text{number of moles} = \frac{\text{mass of sample}}{\text{RFM of the substance}}$$

$$= \frac{60}{40} = 1.5 \text{ moles}$$

Next, we must examine the balanced symbol equation. To make 2 moles of magnesium oxide, we need to use 2 moles of magnesium. Therefore, to make 1.5 moles of magnesium oxide we need to use 1.5 moles of magnesium. Now all we need to do is work out the mass of 1.5 moles of magnesium. We can do this by rearranging our moles equation.

number of moles	×	RFM of the substance	=	mass of the sample
1.5	×	24	=	36 g

This shows that to make 60 g of magnesium oxide, we should burn 36 g of magnesium.

Percentage yield

The amount of product made in a reaction is called the **yield**. Although atoms are never gained or lost during a chemical reaction, we often find that the yield of a reaction is less than the yield that we had predicted. This can be due to a number of reasons:

- The reaction is reversible and does not go to completion.
- Some of the product is lost during filtering, evaporation, when transferring liquids or during heating.
- There may be side-reactions occurring which are producing other products.

The amount of product actually made, compared with the maximum calculated yield, is called the **percentage yield**.

$$\text{Percentage yield} = \frac{\text{actual amount of product}}{\text{calculated maximum yield}} \times 100\%$$

Example

During a chemical reaction, 0.6 g of product is made. The maximum calculated yield is 1.4 g. What is the percentage yield of this reaction?

$$\text{Percentage yield} = \frac{0.6}{1.4} \times 100\%$$

$$= 42.9\%$$

The percentage yield of this reaction is 42.9%. Scientists try to choose reactions with a **high percentage yield** or 'high atom economy'. This contributes towards sustainable development by reducing waste.

QUICK TEST

1. Write down the word equation for the reaction between hydrogen and oxygen.

2. Write down the balanced symbol equation for the reaction between hydrogen and oxygen.

3. What mass of water vapour is produced when 4 g of hydrogen is burnt?

4. What mass of water vapour is produced when 16 g of hydrogen is burnt?

5. What mass of water vapour is produced when 10 g of hydrogen is burnt?

6. Write down the word equation for the reaction between magnesium and oxygen.

7. Write down the balanced symbol equation for the reaction between magnesium and oxygen.

8. What mass of magnesium should be burnt to produce 30 g of magnesium oxide?

9. What mass of magnesium should be burnt to produce 80 g of magnesium oxide?

10. What is the percentage yield of a reaction which has an actual yield of 1.2 g and a theoretical yield of 1.9 g?

Reversible reactions

In science not all reactions go to completion.

Simple reversible reactions

Some chemical reactions are **reversible**: they can proceed in both directions, forwards and backwards. If A and B are **reactants**, and C and D are **products**, a reversible reaction can be summed up as:

$$A + B \rightleftharpoons C + D$$

The two reactants, A and B, can react to make the products C and D, while at the same time, C and D can react together to produce A and B.

If the forward reaction is **exothermic** (gives out energy) then the backwards reaction is **endothermic** (takes in energy). The amount of energy given out by the forwards reaction must be the same as the amount of energy taken in by the backwards reaction.

Copper sulphate reactions

First, the hydrated copper sulphate is heated to make anhydrous copper sulphate. Then, water is added to the anhydrous copper sulphate to produce hydrated copper sulphate.

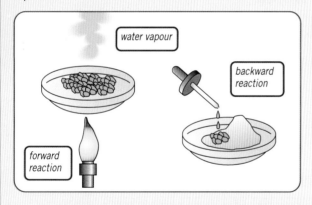

water vapour

backward reaction

forward reaction

? *Hydrated means 'with water': anhydrous means 'without water'.*

In the **forward reaction**, the hydrated copper sulphate takes in energy as it is heated. This is an endothermic reaction.

$$\text{hydrated copper sulphate (blue)} \rightarrow \text{anhydrous copper sulphate (white)} + \text{water}$$

In the **backward reaction**, energy is given out when water is added to the anhydrous copper sulphate. This is an exothermic reaction.

$$\text{anhydrous copper sulphate (white)} + \text{water} \rightarrow \text{hydrated copper sulphate (blue)}$$

Dynamic equilibrium 1

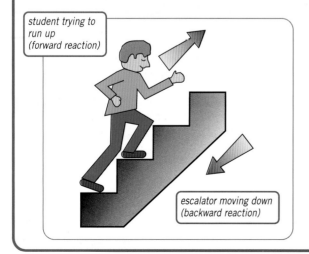

student trying to run up (forward reaction)

escalator moving down (backward reaction)

If a reversible reaction takes place inside a **closed system** (where nothing can enter or leave), a point of equilibrium will eventually be reached. It is a **dynamic equilibrium**, with both the forward and the backward reactions taking place at exactly the same rate. The conditions will affect the position of equilibrium, that is, how much reactant and product are present at equilibrium.

If the forwards reaction is exothermic:

$$\text{reactants} \rightarrow \text{products} + \text{heat}$$

Dynamic equilibrium 2

Increasing the temperature will decrease the amount of product made.

If the forwards reaction is endothermic:

> reactants + heat → products

Increasing the temperature will increase the amount of product made.

> ⚠ *In a dynamic equilibrium, both the forwards and the backwards reaction are still occurring, but as they are occurring at the same rate there is no overall change in the concentrations of the reactants or the products.*

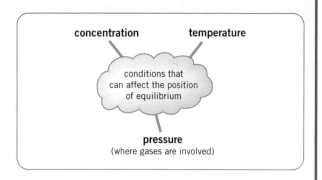

concentration   temperature

conditions that can affect the position of equilibrium

pressure
(where gases are involved)

Reactions involving gases

If a reaction involves gases then the pressure may affect the yield of the reaction.

First, count the number of gas molecules on the left-hand side and the right-hand side of the equation.

> reactants   →   products
> fewer gas molecules → more gas molecules

Increasing the pressure decreases the yield of the product.

> reactants   →   products
> more gas molecules → fewer gas molecules

Increasing the pressure increases the yield of the product.

> reactants   →   products
> same number of → same number of
> gas molecules   gas molecules

Increasing the pressure does not affect the yield of the product.

QUICK TEST

❶ What is special about a reversible reaction?

❷ If a forward reaction gives out energy, what type of reaction is it?

❸ If the backward reaction takes in energy what type of reaction is it?

❹ What can be said about the amount of energy in each case?

❺ What is a closed system?

❻ What is a dynamic equilibrium?

❼ In a reversible reaction the forwards reaction is exothermic. How will increasing the temperature affect the yield of the reaction?

❽ In a reversible reaction the forwards reaction is endothermic. How will increasing the temperature affect the yield of the reaction?

❾ In a reversible reaction the forwards reaction is exothermic. How will decreasing the temperature affect the yield of the reaction?

❿ In a reversible reaction the forwards reaction is endothermic. How will decreasing the temperature affect the yield of the reaction?

The Haber process

The Haber process produces ammonia. Ammonia is made from nitrogen and hydrogen. Hydrogen is obtained from natural gas. Nitrogen is obtained from the fractional distillation of liquid air.

The Haber process

The Haber process is an example of a reversible reaction.

$$N_{2(g)} + 3H_{2(g)} \rightleftharpoons 2NH_{3(g)}$$

Some of the nitrogen and the hydrogen react to form ammonia. At the same time, some of the ammonia breaks down into nitrogen and hydrogen.

This produces a mixture of nitrogen, hydrogen and ammonia gases. Before the ammonia can be sold or used it must be removed from this mixture.

Ammonia has a higher boiling point than nitrogen and hydrogen.

On cooling, the ammonia liquefies and is removed from the reaction mixture. Any unreacted nitrogen and hydrogen can be recycled to cut costs.

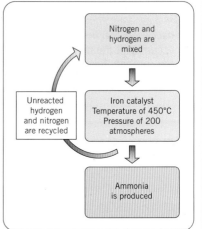

Industrial conditions

The **conditions** are specially chosen. Typical conditions involve:

- a high pressure (200 atmospheres)
- a moderate temperature (450°C)
- an iron **catalyst**.

Choosing the conditions

Pressure

A high pressure is used to increase the amount of ammonia produced. If we look at the balanced symbol equation, there are four gas molecules on the left-hand side of the equation (one nitrogen molecule and three hydrogen molecules), but only two ammonia molecules on the right-hand side of the equation. Increasing the pressure encourages the forward reaction, which increases the amount of ammonia produced because there are fewer gas molecules on the right-hand side of the equation. Ideally, the highest possible pressures should be used. In practice, however, it would be too expensive to build a plant that could withstand pressures greater than 200 atmospheres.

Temperature

The reaction between nitrogen and hydrogen that produces ammonia is exothermic.

A low temperature would increase the yield of ammonia produced at equilibrium. It would, however, also make the rate of the reaction very slow. A higher temperature would give a much faster rate of reaction. The yield of ammonia at equilibrium, however, would be much lower. In practice, a compromise temperature of 450°C is used. This gives an acceptable yield of ammonia, reasonably quickly.

Catalyst

An iron catalyst is used to increase the rate of reaction. This helps to reduce the costs of making ammonia.

Ammonia and fertilisers

Fertilisers replace the essential elements used by plants as they grow. Many fertilisers contain nitrogen, which is needed for **plant growth**. Popular artificial fertilisers include:

- ammonium nitrate
- ammonium phosphate
- ammonium sulphate.

Ammonium nitrate

Ammonia can be oxidised to produce nitric acid. Ammonia gas reacts with oxygen in the air over a platinum catalyst.

$$4NH_3 + 5O_2 \rightarrow 4NO + 6H_2O$$

The nitrogen oxide is cooled and then reacted with water and more oxygen to form nitric acid.

$$4NO + 3O_2 + 2H_2O \rightarrow 4HNO_3$$

The nitric acid can be neutralised with ammonia to make ammonium nitrate.

ammonia + nitric acid → ammonium nitrate

Ammonium phosphate

Ammonia can be neutralised with phosphoric acid to make ammonium phosphate.

ammonia + phosphoric → ammonium
acid phosphate

Ammonium sulphate

Ammonia can be neutralised with sulphuric acid to make ammonium sulphate.

ammonia + sulphuric acid → ammonium
sulphate

QUICK TEST

1. What does the Haber process produce?
2. From where is the hydrogen obtained?
3. From where is the nitrogen obtained?
4. Why could this reaction be described as 'reversible'?
5. Why does increasing the pressure also increase the yield of ammonia?
6. Why is a pressure of 200 atmospheres used?
7. What is the effect of decreasing the temperature on the yield of ammonia?
8. What is the effect of decreasing the temperature on the rate of reaction?
9. Why is a compromise temperature of 450°C used?
10. Name the catalyst used in the reaction.

Rates of reaction

The rate of reaction is either equal to:
- *the amount of reactant used up divided by the time taken*
- *the amount of product made divided by the time taken.*

A chemical reaction can only occur if the reacting particles *collide with enough energy to react*. This is called the *activation energy*. If the particles collide but do not have the minimum energy to react, the particles just bounce apart without reacting.

Analysing rates of reaction

The rate of a chemical reaction can be measured by:
- how fast the products are being made
- how fast the reactants are being used up.

The graph shows the amount of product made in two experiments.

The lines are steepest at the start of the reaction in both experiments. The **lines start to level out as the reactants get used up**. When the line becomes horizontal the reaction has finished.

The graph shows that Experiment 2 has a faster rate of reaction than Experiment 1. Both experiments produce the same amount of product.

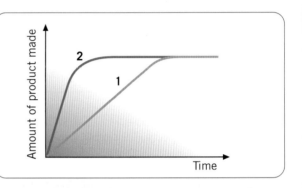

When analysing graphs, remember that the reaction is over when the graph levels out.

Temperature

For a reaction to take place the reactant particles must collide and, when they do collide, have enough energy to react. This is called the activation energy. It is the minimum amount of energy required to **break the bonds and start the reaction**.

At low temperature the rate of reaction slows down
- The particles collide less often
- When they do collide the collisions have less energy

Increasing the temperature increases the rate of reaction because:
- the particles collide more often
- when the particles collide the collisions have more energy.

At higher temperatures the rate of reaction speeds up
- The particles collide more often
- When the particles collide, the collisions have more energy

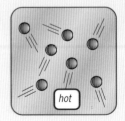

If the temperature is increased, the reactant particles move more quickly.

Increasing the surface area

For a reaction to occur, the particles have to collide.

The greater the surface area:

- the more chance of the reactant particles colliding
- the faster the rate of reaction.

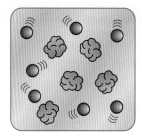

With a large surface area (small pieces) the rate of reaction is higher. The particles collide more often

With a small surface area (large pieces) the rate of reaction is slow. The particles collide less often

Increasing the concentration of dissolved reactants

For a reaction to take place, the reactant particles have to collide.

If the concentration is increased, there will be more reactant particles in the solution. Increasing the concentration increases the rate of reaction because the particles collide more often.

For gases, increasing the pressure has the same effect as increasing the concentration of dissolved particles in solutions.

At a lower concentration the rate of reaction slows down because the particles collide less often

low pressure or concentration

Adding a catalyst

A catalyst increases the rate of reaction, but is not itself used up during the reaction.

Catalysts are specific to certain reactions.

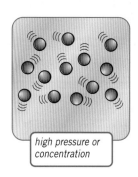

At higher concentration the rate of reaction speeds up because the particles collide more often

high pressure or concentration

The concentration of solutions is given in units of moles per cubic decimetre, mol dm^{-3}.

Equal volumes of solutions of the same molar concentration contain the same number of moles of solute.

QUICK TEST

1. What is the name for the minimum amount of energy required for a reaction to take place?
2. What happens to the rate of reaction if the temperature is decreased?
3. What happens to the rate of reaction if the concentration of reactants is increased?
4. What happens to the rate of reaction if the pressure of gaseous reactants is increased?
5. What happens to the rate of reaction if the surface area of reactants is increased?
6. How does a catalyst affect the rate of reaction?
7. Why can catalysts be reused?
8. How can the rate of reaction be measured?
9. How could you increase the rate of reaction?
10. Iron is a catalyst in the Haber process. Will it be a catalyst for other reactions?

Exothermic and endothermic reactions

During chemical reactions, old bonds are broken and new bonds are made. *Energy* is required to break bonds, while energy is released when new bonds are formed. If, overall, energy is supplied to the surroundings, we say that the reaction is *exothermic*. If energy is taken from the surroundings, we say that the reaction is *endothermic*.

Energy changes and chemical reactions

During chemical reactions, overall energy can be either:

■ **taken from the surroundings**
■ **given to the surroundings.**

This **energy** can be in the form of:

■ heat
■ light
■ sound
■ electricity.

Exothermic reactions

In exothermic reactions, energy is given out to the surroundings. This energy is normally in the form of heat, so this causes a rise in temperature. Burning 'gas' is an example of an exothermic reaction.

Endothermic reactions

In endothermic reactions, energy, usually in the form of heat, is taken in from the surroundings. This is often shown by a decrease in the temperature. The thermal decomposition of limestone is an example of an endothermic reaction. A lot of heat must be taken in for the reaction to take place.

Bond energy calculations 1

Each chemical bond has a specific '**bond energy**'. This is the amount of energy that must be taken in to break one mole of bonds.

Bond	Bond energy (kJ mol^{-1})
C–H	413
O=O	496
C=O	743
O–H	463
C–O	358

Example

Burning the fuel methane, CH_4

$$H-\overset{\overset{\displaystyle H}{|}}{\underset{\underset{\displaystyle H}{|}}{C}}-H \;+\; \begin{matrix} O=O \\ O=O \end{matrix} \;\rightarrow\; O=C=O \;+\; \begin{matrix} H\diagdown^{O}\diagup H \\ H\diagdown_{O}\diagup H \end{matrix}$$

Energy taken in to break the bonds:

■ 4 moles of C–H = 4 x 413 = 1652 kJ mol^{-1}
■ 2 moles of O=O = 2 x 496 = 992 kJ mol^{-1}
■ Total = 1652 + 992 = 2644 kJ mol^{-1}

Energy given out when forming bonds:

■ 2 moles of C=O = 2 × 743 = 1486 kJ mol^{-1}
■ 4 moles of O–H = 4 × 463 = 1852 kJ mol^{-1}
■ Total = 1486 + 1852 = 3338 kJ mol^{-1}

Difference in energy, that is, between energy given out and the energy taken in:

$$= 3338 \text{ kJ mol}^{-1} - 2644 \text{ kJ mol}^{-1}$$
$$= 694 \text{ kJ mol}^{-1}$$

This reaction gives out more energy than it takes in and so it is exothermic.

Bond energy calculations 2

In an exothermic reaction, the products have less energy than the reactants.

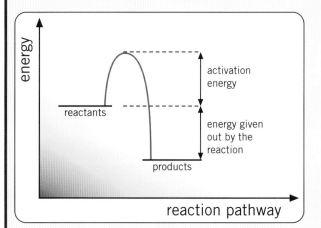

The difference in energy between the products and the reactants is the amount of energy given out by the reaction. The activation energy is the amount of energy needed to get the reaction started. This energy is required to break the bonds in the reactants.

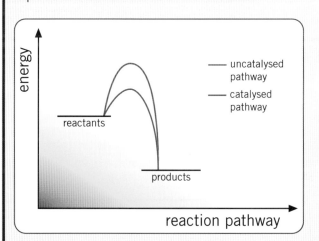

Catalysts provide an alternative reaction pathway that has lower activation energy. More reactant particles will have the lower activation energy and so catalysed reactions happen faster.

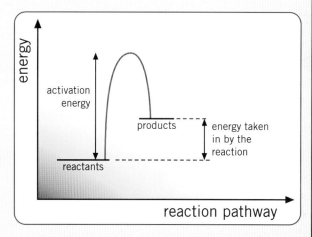

In an endothermic reaction, the products have more energy than the reactants.

The difference in energy between the products and the reactants is the amount of energy taken in by the reaction.

The burning of fuels is always exothermic. During exothermic reactions energy is transferred to the surroundings.

QUICK TEST

1. During a chemical reaction, the temperature increases. What sort of reaction has taken place?

2. How do we know that the decomposition of limestone is an endothermic reaction?

3. How do you know that burning coal is an exothermic reaction?

4. When hydrochloric acid neutralises sodium hydroxide, the temperature increases. Is this an exothermic reaction or an endothermic reaction?

5. Do all exothermic reactions release energy in the form of heat?

6. If a bond is broken, is energy released or supplied?

7. What is the 'bond energy'?

8. Is energy released or supplied when a bond is formed?

9. When we burn fuels, do we expect the reaction to be exothermic or endothermic?

10. Methanol has the formula CH_3OH.

```
      H
      |
  H - C - O - H
      |
      H
```

How much energy must be supplied to break the bonds in one mole of methanol?

Electrolysis of sodium chloride solution

Sodium chloride is an ionic compound formed from the combination of a group 1 metal (sodium) and a group 7 non-metal (chlorine).

Sodium chloride

Sodium chloride (common salt) is an important resource. It is dissolved in large quantities in seawater, and is also found in vast underground deposits, which formed as ancient seas evaporated. Rock salt (unpurified salt) is often used on icy roads. The salt lowers the freezing point of water from 0°C to about −5°C. Sprinkling rock salt on roads means that any water present will not freeze and form ice unless the temperature is very low. A solution of sodium chloride in water is called **brine**.

The electrolysis of concentrated sodium chloride solution is an important industrial process.

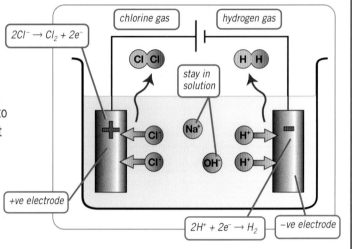

chlorine gas   hydrogen gas

$2Cl^- \rightarrow Cl_2 + 2e^-$

stay in solution

+ve electrode

$2H^+ + 2e^- \rightarrow H_2$

−ve electrode

Electrolysis

During electrolysis, the ions move towards the oppositely charged electrode. The electrolysis of sodium chloride solution produces three useful products.

During electrolysis, pairs of hydrogen ions, H^+ ions, are attracted to the **negative electrode**, where they pick up electrons to form hydrogen molecules, H_2.

> hydrogen ions + electrons → hydrogen molecules
> $$2H^+ \quad + \quad 2e^- \quad \rightarrow \quad H_2$$

Pairs of chloride ions, Cl^- ions, are attracted to the **positive electrode**, where they deposit electrons to form chlorine molecules.

> chloride ions − electrons → chlorine molecules
> $$2Cl^- \quad - \quad 2e^- \quad \rightarrow \quad Cl_2$$

A solution of sodium hydroxide, NaOH, is also produced. Each of these products can be used to make other useful materials.

Oxidation and reduction

In the electrolysis of concentrated sodium chloride solution:
- **hydrogen ions are reduced to hydrogen molecules**
- **chloride ions are oxidised to chlorine molecules.**

Reduction reactions happen when a species gains electrons. Here, two hydrogen ions both gain an electron to form a hydrogen molecule.

Oxidation reactions occur when a species loses electrons. Here, two chloride ions both lose an electron to form a chlorine molecule.

Reduction and oxidation reactions must always occur together and so are sometimes referred to as **redox** reactions.

Useful products from the electrolysis of sodium chloride solution

Chlorine

Chlorine is used:
- to make bleach
- to sterilise water
- to produce hydrochloric acid
- in the production of PVC.

Hydrogen

Hydrogen is used in the manufacture of margarine.

Sodium hydroxide

Sodium hydroxide is an alkali used in paper making and in the manufacture of many products including:
- soaps and detergents
- rayon and acetate fibres.

Electrolysis of molten sodium chloride

Solid sodium chloride does not conduct electricity because the ions cannot move. If sodium chloride is heated until it becomes molten, however, the **sodium ions and chloride ions are able to move and electrolysis can occur**. During the electrolysis of molten sodium chloride, the ions move **towards the oppositely charged electrodes**. Sodium, Na^+ ions are attracted to the negative electrode where they pick up electrons to form sodium, Na atoms.

> sodium ion + electron → sodium atom
> $$Na^+ + e^- \rightarrow Na$$

Pairs of chloride ions, Cl^- ions are attracted to the positive electrode, where they deposit electrons to form chlorine molecules.

> chloride ions – electrons → chlorine molecules
> $$2Cl^- - 2e^- \rightarrow Cl_2$$

Electrolysis of molten lead iodide

If lead iodide is heated until it becomes molten, the lead ions and iodide ions can move. During electrolysis lead, Pb^{2+} ions are attracted to the negative electrode, where they pick up electrons to form lead atoms.

> lead ion + 2 electrons → lead atom
> $$Pb^{2+} + 2e^- \rightarrow Pb$$

Pairs of iodide ions, I^- ions are attracted to the positive electrode, where they deposit electrons to form iodine molecules.

> iodide ions – electrons → iodine molecules
> $$2I^- - 2e^- \rightarrow I_2$$

QUICK TEST

1. What groups do sodium and chlorine belong to?
2. Where is sodium chloride found?
3. Why are roads 'salted'?
4. What is brine?
5. During the electrolysis of brine, what is produced at the positive electrode?
6. During the electrolysis of brine, what is produced at the negative electrode?
7. Which other useful chemical is produced?
8. How is chlorine used?
9. How is hydrogen used?
10. How is sodium hydroxide used?

Acids, bases and neutralisation

Acids and **bases** are chemical opposites. Some bases dissolve in water and are called *alkalis*.

Weak and strong acids

Acidic solutions have a pH of less than 7.

Some acids are described as strong. Examples of strong acids include:

- hydrochloric acid
- sulphuric acid
- nitric acid.

Strong acids are **completely ionised in water**. When hydrochloric acid is placed in water, every hydrogen chloride molecule splits up to form hydrogen ions and chloride ions.

$$HCl \rightarrow H^+ + Cl^-$$

Other acids are described as weak acids. Examples of weak acids include:

- ethanoic acid (also known as acetic acid)
- citric acid
- carbonic acid.

Weak acids do not completely ionise in water. When ethanoic acid is placed in water, only a small fraction of the ethanoic acid molecules split up to form hydrogen ions and ethanoate ions.

$$CH_3COOH \rightarrow H^+ + CH_3COO^-$$

Weak and strong alkalis

Alkaline solutions have a pH of more than 7.

Some alkalis are described as strong alkalis. Examples of strong alkalis include:

- sodium hydroxide
- potassium hydroxide.

Strong alkalis are completely ionised in water. When sodium hydroxide is placed in water, it splits up to form sodium ions and hydroxide ions.

$$NaOH \rightarrow Na^+ + OH^-$$

Other alkalis are described as weak. Examples of weak alkalis include ammonia.

Weak alkalis do not completely ionise in water. Ammonia is a weak alkali which produces hydroxide, OH^- ions, when it reacts with water.

$$\text{ammonia} + \text{water} \rightarrow \text{ammonium ion} + \text{hydroxide ion}$$
$$NH_3 + H_2O \rightarrow NH_4^+ + OH^-$$

Ammonium salts are useful fertilisers.

The pH scale

The **pH scale** can be used to distinguish between weak and strong acids and alkalis.

It measures the concentration of hydrogen ions. Neutral solutions have a pH of 7. Acidic solutions have a pH of less than 7. The strongest acids have a pH of 1. Many foods, such as lemons, contain acids. These foods taste sour. If water is added to an acid it becomes more dilute and less corrosive.

Alkaline solutions have a pH of more than 7. The strongest alkalis have a pH of 14.

Many cleaning materials contain alkalis. If water is added to an alkali it becomes more dilute and less corrosive.

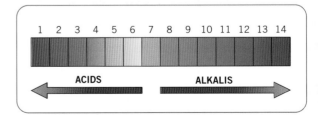

Indicators

Indicators can be used to show the pH of a solution. They work by changing colour.

Naming salts

Neutralising hydrochloric acid will produce chloride salts.

hydrochloric acid	+	sodium hydroxide	→	sodium chloride	+	water
hydrochloric acid	+	calcium hydroxide	→	calcium chloride	+	water

Neutralising nitric acid will produce nitrate salts.

nitric acid	+	potassium hydroxide	→	potassium nitrate	+	water
nitric acid	+	calcium hydroxide	→	calcium nitrate	+	water

Neutralising sulphuric acid will produce sulphate salts.

sulphuric acid	+	sodium hydroxide	→	sodium sulphate	+	water
sulphuric acid	+	potassium hydroxide	→	potassium sulphate	+	water

💡 **Ammonia reacts with water to form a weak alkali. Ammonia solution can be neutralised with acids to form ammonium salts.**

Neutralisation reactions

The reaction between an acid and a base is called **neutralisation**. Acidic solutions contain hydrogen, H+ ions. Alkaline solutions contain hydroxide, OH– ions.

The reaction between an acid and an alkali can be shown by the equation:

$$\text{acid} + \text{alkali} \rightarrow \text{salt} + \text{water}$$
$$H^+ + OH^- \rightarrow H_2O$$

The type of salt produced during the reaction depends on:
- **the alkali used**
- **the acid used.**

Wasp and bee stings are painful.

A wasp sting is alkaline. The pain can be reduced by applying vinegar (an acid) to the sting.

A bee sting is acidic. This time the pain can be reduced by applying an alkali like camomile lotion.

QUICK TEST

1. What ions are found in acidic solutions?
2. What ions are found in alkaline solutions?
3. Name three strong acids.
4. Why are some acids strong?
5. Name three weak acids
6. Name a weak alkali.
7. Why are some alkalis weak?
8. What does the pH scale measure?
9. Name the salt formed by the reaction between hydrochloric acid and potassium hydroxide.
10. Name the salt formed by the reaction between nitric acid and potassium hydroxide.

Making salts

Salts are very important materials. Salts can be used:

- in the production of fertilisers
- in the production of fireworks
- as colouring agents.

Making salts from metal carbonates

We have already seen how metal hydroxides can be neutralised by acids to form salts and water.

> metal hydroxide + acid $\longrightarrow$ salt + water

Metal carbonates can also be neutralised by acids to form salts. Most metal carbonates are **insoluble**, so they are **bases**, but they are not **alkalis**. When metal carbonates are neutralised, salts, water and carbon dioxide are produced.

The general equation for the reaction is:

> metal carbonate + acid $\longrightarrow$ salt + water + carbon dioxide

Examples

> zinc carbonate + sulphuric acid $\longrightarrow$ zinc sulphate + water + carbon dioxide
>
> $ZnCO_3 + H_2SO_4 \longrightarrow ZnSO_4 + H_2O + CO_2$

> copper carbonate + hydrochloric acid $\longrightarrow$ copper chloride + water + carbon dioxide
>
> $CuCO_3 + 2HCl \longrightarrow CuCl_2 + H_2O + CO_2$

This diagram shows how copper chloride salt is made.

The steps involved in the production of copper chloride are as follows:

- Copper carbonate is added to hydrochloric acid until all the acid is used up.
- Any unreacted copper carbonate is **filtered off**.
- The solution of copper chloride and water is poured into an evaporating basin.
- The basin is **heated gently** until the first crystals of copper chloride start to appear.
- The solution is then left on a warm windowsill or near a radiator for a few days to allow the remaining copper chloride to **crystallise**.

Sulphuric acid is neutralised to form sulphate salts. Hydrochloric acid is neutralised to form chloride salts. Nitric acid is neutralised to form nitrate salts.

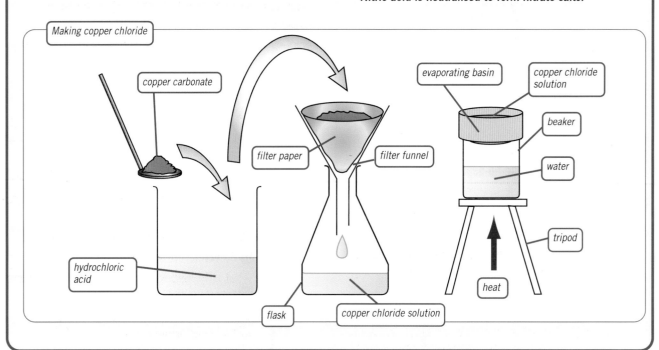

Making copper chloride

copper carbonate

filter paper

filter funnel

evaporating basin

copper chloride solution

beaker

water

tripod

hydrochloric acid

heat

flask

copper chloride solution

Metals

Fairly reactive metals can be reacted with acids to form a salt and hydrogen.

Salts of very unreactive metals such as copper cannot be made in this way because these metals do not react with acids.

Salts of very reactive metals like sodium cannot be made in this way because the reaction between the metal and acid is too vigorous to be carried out safely.

Examples

zinc + hydrochloric acid → zinc chloride + hydrogen

$Zn + 2HCl \rightarrow ZnCl_2 + H_2$

magnesium + sulphuric acid → magnesium sulphate + hydrogen

$Mg + H_2SO_4 \rightarrow MgSO_4 + H_2$

Metal oxides

Metal oxides are also bases. They can be reacted with acids to make salts and water.

metal oxide + acid → salt + water

Examples

copper oxide + hydrochloric acid → copper chloride + water

$CuO + 2HCl \rightarrow CuCl_2 + H_2O$

zinc oxide + sulphuric acid → zinc sulphate + water

$ZnO + H_2SO_4 \rightarrow ZnSO_4 + H_2O$

Precipitation reactions

Some insoluble salts can be made from the reaction between two solutions. Barium sulphate is an insoluble salt. It can be made by the reaction between solutions of barium chloride and sodium sulphate.

barium chloride + sodium sulphate → barium sulphate + sodium chloride

$BaCl_{2(aq)} + Na_2SO_{4(aq)} \rightarrow BaSO_{4(s)} + 2NaCl_{(aq)}$

The insoluble barium sulphate can be filtered off, washed and dried.

The two original salts, barium chloride and sodium sulphate, have swapped partners. This can be described as a double decomposition reaction. The chloride ions and sodium ions are **spectator ions**. They are present, but not involved in the reaction.

QUICK TEST

1. What is formed when hydrochloric acid reacts with potassium hydroxide?
2. What is formed when sulphuric acid reacts with sodium hydroxide?
3. Which gas is given off when metal carbonates react with acids?
4. What is formed when hydrochloric acid reacts with zinc carbonate?
5. What is formed when sulphuric acid reacts with magnesium carbonate?
6. How could you get a sample of a soluble salt?
7. What is formed when hydrochloric acid reacts with magnesium?
8. What is formed when sulphuric acid reacts with zinc?
9. What is formed when hydrochloric acid reacts with zinc oxide?
10. What is formed when sulphuric acid reacts with copper oxide?

Chemical tests

In the practice of chemistry, we often wish to identify chemicals.

Gas tests

Carbon dioxide

What do you do?

The gas is bubbled through limewater.

What happens?

The limewater turns cloudy.

Carbonates react with acids to produce **carbon dioxide**.

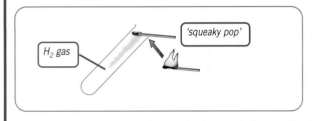

Hydrogen

What do you do?

A lighted splint is placed nearby.

What happens?

The hydrogen burns with a squeaky pop.

Chlorine

What do you do?

Place damp litmus paper in the gas.

What happens?

The litmus paper is bleached.

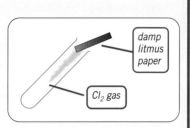

Oxygen

What do you do?

A glowing splint is placed in the gas.

What happens?

The splint relights.

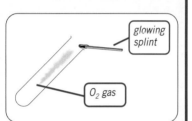

Ammonia

What do you do?

Place damp red litmus paper in the gas.

What happens?

The damp red litmus paper turns blue.

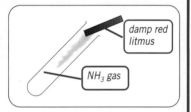

Flame tests

Flame tests can be used to identify some metals present in salts.

What do you do?

Clean a flame test wire by placing it into the hottest part of a Bunsen flame.

Dip the end of the wire into water and then into the salt sample.

Hold the salt into the hottest part of the flame and observe the colour seen.

What happens?

lithium – red
sodium – orange
potassium – lilac

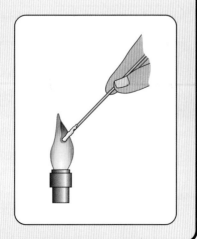

Carbonates

Carbonates react with acids to form carbon dioxide.

When copper carbonate is heated, it decomposes to form copper oxide and carbon dioxide. This can be identified by a distinctive colour change: **copper carbonate is green and copper oxide is black**.

When zinc carbonate is heated it decomposes to form zinc oxide and carbon dioxide. This can also be identified by a distinctive colour change: **zinc carbonate is white, while zinc oxide is yellow when hot but as it cools it turns white**.

Hydroxide tests

We can identify other metals by adding sodium hydroxide solution to solutions of the salt. If the unknown metal forms an **insoluble precipitate**, we can use the colour of the precipitate to identify the metal present.

copper (II) – pale blue precipitate

iron (II) – green precipitate

iron (III) – brown precipitate

Precipitation reactions

Some insoluble salts can be made from the reaction between two solutions. **This test is used to detect the presence of sulphate ions.**

Barium sulphate is an insoluble salt. It can be made by the reaction between solutions containing barium ions and **sulphate ions**, for example:

barium chloride + sodium sulphate → barium sulphate + sodium chloride

$$BaCl_{2(aq)} + Na_2SO_{4(aq)} \rightarrow BaSO_{4(s)} + 2NaCl_{(aq)}$$

The insoluble barium sulphate can be filtered off, washed and dried. The two original salts, barium chloride and sodium sulphate, have swapped partners. This can be described as a double decomposition reaction. The chloride ions and sodium ions are **spectator ions**. They are present, but they are not involved in the reaction.

Testing for halide ions

We can test for the presence of **halide** ions by **adding silver nitrate and dilute nitric acid** to the sample being tested. The colour of the precipitate formed reveals which halide ion is present.

- A white precipitate of silver chloride indicates that chloride ions are present.
- A cream precipitate of silver bromide indicates that bromide ions are present.
- A yellow precipitate of silver iodide indicates that iodide ions are present.

QUICK TEST

1. What is the test for carbon dioxide?
2. What is the test for chlorine?
3. What is the test for oxygen?
4. What is the test for hydrogen?
5. Which gas is produced when carbonates react with acid?
6. What is the colour of copper carbonate?
7. During a flame test what colour is given by a potassium salt?
8. During a flame test what colour is given by a sodium salt?
9. What colour precipitate is formed when a solution of an iron (II) salt reacts with sodium hydroxide?
10. What colour precipitate is formed when a solution of a copper (II) salt reacts with sodium hydroxide?

Water

Have you ever noticed that water from other parts of the country can sometimes taste different? This is because substances are dissolved in the water.

The water cycle

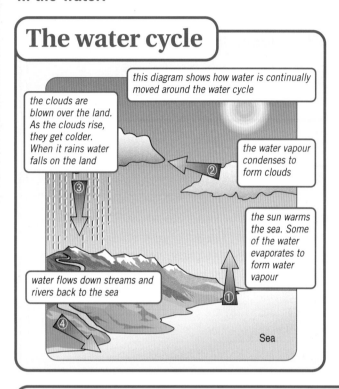

this diagram shows how water is continually moved around the water cycle

the clouds are blown over the land. As the clouds rise, they get colder. When it rains water falls on the land

② the water vapour condenses to form clouds

① the sun warms the sea. Some of the water evaporates to form water vapour

water flows down streams and rivers back to the sea

Sea

Purifying water

Only appropriate locations, far away from polluted areas, are chosen as sources of drinking water. In the United Kingdom our **resources** are found in:

■ lakes
■ rivers
■ aquifer (rock formations that contain water)
■ reservoirs.

The water is first **filtered** to remove solid impurities. Finally, **chlorine** is added to kill most of the microorganisms found in water. These tiny organisms can multiply quickly and cause disease, so their levels must be brought down to acceptable levels.

Problems with nitrate fertilisers

Nitrate **fertilisers** can cause problems if they are washed into lakes or streams. Algae (small plants) thrive in the fertiliser-rich water and grow very well.

Eventually, the algae die and bacteria start to decompose (break down) the algae. As the algae are decomposed, all the oxygen in the water is used up. Fish and other aquatic life cannot get enough oxygen and so they die.

This process is called **eutrophication**.

Nitrate fertilisers can also find their way into our drinking water supplies. There have been health concerns over the levels of nitrate found in water and a

possible link to a prevalence of stomach cancer and 'blue baby' disease.

Babies suffering from blue baby disease have elevated levels of nitrates in their blood. These nitrates reduce the amount of oxygen that the blood can carry, and so the baby's skin looks blue. Although no firm links have yet been established, it seems wise to limit the levels of nitrate in drinking water until more is known.

Water can also be polluted by:
■ lead compounds from lead pipes
■ pesticides that have been sprayed near the water resources, such as reservoirs.

Solubility

Water has many uses including as:
■ a coolant ■ a raw material ■ a **solvent**.

Water is a particularly **good solvent and dissolves most ionic compounds**. We can measure the solubility of a substance, called the solute, in water by measuring the

number of grams of the substance that will dissolve in 100 g of water. The more grams of the substance that dissolve, the more soluble the substance is. Generally, the higher the temperature of the water, the more soluble a substance will become.

Detergents

Washing powders and washing-up liquids contain chemicals called **detergents**.

Detergents molecules have two parts.

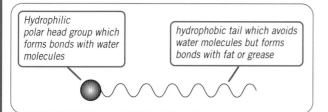

Hydrophilic polar head group which forms bonds with water molecules

hydrophobic tail which avoids water molecules but forms bonds with fat or grease

Many detergent molecules form a sphere around the grease or fat, which can then be washed off.

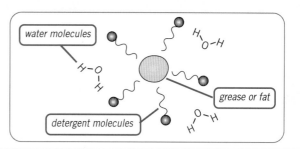

water molecules

grease or fat

detergent molecules

Washing powders

We use washing powders to get clothes clean. They consist of many ingredients, including:

■ a **detergent** to get rid of dirt
■ water softeners to remove the hardness from hard water, in order that the detergent can work properly
■ bleaches to remove stains
■ enzymes that help to remove stains at low temperatures
■ optical brighteners to make the clothes look clean.

Every item of clothing contains a washing label, displaying symbols that indicate the **washing conditions** needed to clean the garment.

The bars under the 'washtub' display the washing conditions that should be used, and the temperature of the label indicates the maximum temperature at which the clothing should be washed.

Washing clothes at a lower temperature than the one indicated on the label will save money but might not get the clothing clean.

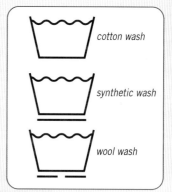

cotton wash

synthetic wash

wool wash

However, today's more advanced washing powders endeavour to clean clothes, even at low temperatures. This helps **people to save both energy and money**.

Dry cleaning

Some **fabrics can be damaged by washing** them in water. These fabrics should be dry cleaned. As the name 'dry cleaning' suggests, no water is involved in the process. A different solvent, such as perchloroethylene, is used. First, the clothes are washed in the solvent. The solvent is then extracted so it can be used again. Finally, the clothes are pressed.

Some clothes may be damaged by **stains which do not dissolve in water**. The stains do not dissolve in water because the forces of attraction between the stain molecules are stronger than the forces of attraction between stain molecules and water molecules. However, these clothes can be cleaned using dry cleaning. The stains dissolve during dry cleaning because the forces of attraction between the dry cleaning solvent molecules and the stain molecules are stronger than the forces of attraction between the stain molecules.

QUICK TEST

1. How are solid impurities removed from drinking water?
2. How are microorganisms removed from drinking water?
3. What is the name of the problem caused by nitrate fertilisers entering lakes?
4. List three ways in which water can be polluted.

Uses of oils and alcohol

Plant oils are a valuable source of energy in our diets. They are also essential sources of vitamins A and D. If we eat too many vegetable oils, however, we could suffer from health problems, such as heart disease, in later life.

Vegetable oils

Vegetable oils can be produced from the **fruits, seeds or nuts** of some plants. Popular vegetable oils include olive oil and sunflower oil.

vegetable oils can be extracted from the fruits, seeds and nuts of some plants. The oil is removed by crushing up the plant material and collecting the oil

Using fats for cooking

Fats have **higher boiling points** than water. Cooking food by frying is, therefore, much faster than cooking food by boiling. In addition, frying foods produces interesting **new flavours** and **increases the energy content** of the food.

frying potatoes to make chips

What is a fat molecule?

Fats and oils are complex molecules.

this is a molecule of a common animal fat

Saturated and unsaturated fats

Animal fats are usually **solid**, or nearly solid, at room temperature. They are **saturated fats**. A saturated fat contains many C—C bonds but no **C═C** bonds. Scientists believe that people who eat lots of saturated fats may develop raised blood cholesterol levels. This is linked with an increased risk of heart disease.

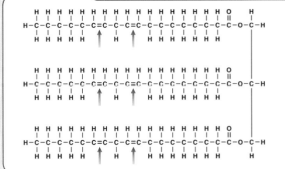

this is a molecule of a common vegetable oil

Most vegetable fats are liquids at room temperature and so are described as oils.

Vegetable oils contain C═C bonds. Scientists describe these molecules as **unsaturated fats** because they could hold more hydrogen atoms. The presence of the C═C bonds affects the way that the fatty acids in the molecule can pack together. C═C bonds are rigid and their presence causes kinks so that the fatty acids cannot pack closely together. Unsaturated fats have **lower melting points** than saturated fats. While most vegetable fats are **liquid at room temperature**, most animal fats are solids.

Polyunsaturated fats

Some unsaturated fats have just one C=C bond in the fatty acid chain. These are described as mono-unsaturated fats. Other unsaturated fats have **many** **C=C bonds**. These are known as **polyunsaturated fats**. Scientists believe that polyunsaturated fats are better for people's health.

Hydrogenated vegetable oils

Vegetable oils are often liquids at room temperature because they contain C=C bonds. There are, however, advantages to using fats that are solid at room temperature. They are easier to spread and can be used to make new products like cakes and pastries. Vegetable oils can be made solid at room temperature by a process known as **hydrogenation**. The oils are heated with **hydrogen and a nickel catalyst**. The hydrogen atoms add across double bonds to form fats that are solid at room temperature. In addition, **hydrogenated** vegetable oils have a longer shelf life.

margarine is one example of a hydrogenated vegetable oil

Industrial alcohol

Traditionally, alcohol has been made by fermentation. However, there is now another way of producing vast amounts of alcohol. In this method, **ethene** (which is produced during the cracking of long chain hydrocarbons) is **reacted with steam to produce ethanol**.

A catalyst of **phosphoric acid and a temperature of 300°C** are used. This method of producing ethanol is much cheaper than fermentation. Our reserves of fossil fuels are, however, finite and will run out one day.

$$\text{ethene} + \text{steam} \rightarrow \text{ethanol}$$
$$C_2H_4 + H_2O \rightarrow C_2H_5OH$$

QUICK TEST

1. Which parts of plants can we obtain oils from?
2. Which part of a sunflower is used to obtain oil?
3. Which vitamins do we obtain from eating fats?
4. Why is frying food faster than boiling food?
5. Will a food that has been fried or a food that has been boiled contain more energy?
6. If a fat is a solid at room temperature, would you expect it to be saturated or unsaturated?
7. What do polyunsaturated fats have?
8. What are the advantages of having fats that are solid at room temperature?
9. What is the catalyst used in the hydrogenation of vegetable oil to produce margarine?
10. What is the name of the catalyst that is used in the industrial production of ethanol?

Practice questions

Use the questions to test your progress. Check your answers on page 126.

1. The table below shows the names of four different salts.

Name of salt
copper chloride
zinc sulphate
sodium nitrate
insoluble barium sulphate

Four different methods have been used to make these salts.
A different method was chosen for each salt.

a) Which salt was made by the reaction between a metal and an acid? ....

b) Which salt was made by the reaction between a metal hydroxide and a salt? ....

c) Which salt is made by a precipitation reaction? ....

d) Which salt was made by the reaction between a metal oxide and an acid? ....

2. The electrolysis of lead chloride can be used to produce lead and chlorine.

a) Why must the lead chloride be molten during electrolysis? ....

b) Give the balanced symbol equation for the reaction that takes place at the negative electrode. ....

c) Give the balanced symbol equation for the reaction that takes place at the positive electrode. ....

3. The table below is about different substances.

Substance	Information about the substance
A	consists of molecules which are made from a few atoms
B	contains huge numbers of carbon atoms which are all joined together by strong covalent bonds
C	contains huge numbers of silicon and oxygen atoms which are all joined together by strong covalent bonds
D	is a compound which dissolves in water

a) What is the name of substance B? ....

b) Which of these substances could be methane? ....

c) Which of these substances could be a solution of sodium hydroxide? ....

d) Which of these substances is an ionic compound? ....

e) Which of these substances consists of simple molecules? ....

f) Which two substances have a giant covalent structure? ....

g) Will substance B dissolve in water? ....

Particle	Information about the particle
A	These particles are found in atoms and have a charge of 1−.
B	These particles are found in atoms and have no charge.
C	These particles are found in atoms and have a charge of 1+ and a mass of one atomic mass unit.

4. The table below is about the particles found in atoms.

a) What is the name of particle A? ....

b) Which of these particles are found in shells? ....

c) Which of these substances has a negligible mass? ....

d) Which of these substances is a proton? ....

e) What is the mass of particle B? ....

f) Which two particles are found in the nucleus? ....

g) The mass number is equal to the sum of the numbers of which two particles? ....

h) The atomic number of an atom is the same as the number of which two particles? ....

5. The electrolysis of concentrated sodium chloride solution produces three useful products:

chlorine

hydrogen

sodium hydroxide

a) Give the balanced symbol equation for the reaction that takes place at the negative electrode. ....

b) Give the balanced symbol for the reaction that takes place at the positive electrode. ....

c) Give one important use of chlorine. ....

6. Chlorine is a more reactive halogen than bromine.

a) What safety precautions should be taken when using chlorine? ....

b) Write the word equation for the reaction between chlorine and potassium bromide. ....

c) Write the balanced symbol equation for the reaction between chlorine and potassium bromide. ....

7. The table below is about atoms of different elements.

Element	Information about the element
A	Atoms of this element have one electron in their outer shell.
B	Atoms of this element have seven electrons in their outer shell.
C	Atoms of this element have a full outer shell of electrons.
D	These elements are found in the centre of the periodic table.

a) Which of these elements could be copper? ....

b) Which of these elements is in group 7? ....

c) Which of these elements forms diatomic molecules? ....

d) Which of these elements could be neon? ....

e) Which of these elements could be sodium? ....

f) Which of these elements is a halogen? ....

g) Which of these elements is a transition metal? ....

h) Which of these atoms reacts to form ions which have a 1+ charge? ....

i) Which of these elements will not react? ....

j) Which of these elements could react with chlorine to form a white compound that would dissolve to form a colourless solution? ....

8. During a chemical reaction 0.8 g of product is made. The maximum calculated yield is 2.2 g.

a) What is the percentage yield of this reaction? ....

b) Suggest why the actual yield is lower than the calculated yield for this reaction. ....

Speed, velocity and acceleration

The *speed* or *velocity* of an object is a measure of how fast it is moving.

How to calculate speed and velocity

To find the speed of an object, we need to know how far it has travelled and how long it took to travel this **distance**. We then use the equation:

$$\text{speed} = \frac{\text{distance}}{\text{time}} \text{ or } v = \frac{d}{t}$$

We can write this equation as a formula triangle. We now cover, with our finger, the quantity the question is asking us to calculate. The triangle shows us the formula we should use.

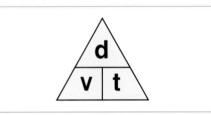

Example

A sprinter runs 400 m in 50 s. Calculate his speed.

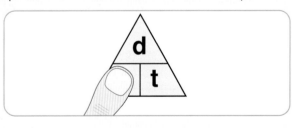

$$v = \frac{d}{t} = \frac{400 \text{ m}}{50 \text{ s}} = 8 \text{ m/s}$$

💡 *Remember to include the correct units with all your answers or you will lose marks.*

Example

After being hit, a cricket ball travels at 50 m/s for 2 s. How far has the ball travelled?

Using the formula triangle we can see that:

distance = speed × time or d = v × t

d = v × t = 50 m/s × 2 s = 100 m

Example

A car travels 200 km at an average speed of 40 km/h. How long does the journey take?

Using the formula triangle we see that:

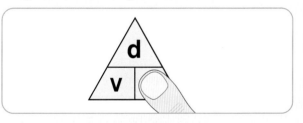

$$\text{time} = \frac{\text{distance}}{\text{speed}} \text{ or } t = \frac{d}{v}$$

$$t = \frac{d}{v} = \frac{200 \text{ km}}{40 \text{ km/h}} = 5 \text{ h}$$

Speed and velocity

We often use the words speed and velocity as if they have the same meaning. There is, however, a small but important difference between the two words.

■ A **speed** tells us **how fast an object is moving**.

■ A **velocity** tells us **how fast an object is moving and in which direction**.

So, for example, 20 m/s is a speed, 20 m/s northwards is a velocity.

Acceleration

If an object is **changing its speed** or **its velocity**, it is **accelerating**. The **acceleration** of an object tells us **how rapidly its speed is changing**.

A motorcyclist has an acceleration of 20 km/h/s. This means his speed is increasing by 20 km/h each second.

A rocket has an acceleration of 50 m/s/s (more usually written as 50 m/s^2). This means that the rocket is increasing its speed by 50 m/s every second.

To calculate the acceleration of an object, we need to know by how much its speed or velocity has changed and how long this change in velocity has taken.

We then use the equation:

$$\text{acceleration} = \frac{\text{change in velocity}}{\text{time taken}} = \frac{\Delta v}{t}$$

Here, the Δ symbol (Greek letter 'delta') means 'change in'.

Example

A racing car accelerates from rest to a speed of 100 m/s in just 5 s. Calculate the acceleration of the car.

$$a = \frac{\Delta v}{t} = \frac{100 \text{ m/s}}{5 \text{ s}} = 20 \text{ m/s}^2$$

Example

This bobsleigh team is about to increase its speed from 0 m/s to 50 m/s in 10 s. Calculate its acceleration.

$$a = \frac{\Delta v}{t} = \frac{50 \text{ m/s}}{10 \text{ s}} = 5 \text{ m/s}^2$$

Using the formula triangle we can see that:

$$\Delta v = a \times t$$

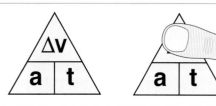

Example

Calculate the change in velocity of an aircraft that accelerates at 20 m/s^2 for 10 s.

$$\Delta v = a \times t = 20 \text{ m/s}^2 \times 10 \text{ s} = 200 \text{ m/s}$$

Also:

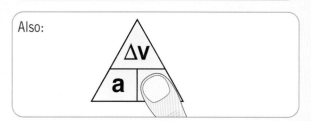

so:

$$t = \frac{\Delta v}{a}$$

Example

Calculate the time it would take for a car to increase its velocity from 10 m/s to 60 m/s if its acceleration is 5 m/s^2.

$$t = \frac{\Delta v}{a} = \frac{50 \text{ m/s}}{5 \text{ m/s}^2} = 10 \text{ s}$$

💡 *Practise using the formula triangle. It is very useful for lots of formulas you will need in your exams.*

QUICK TEST

1. Calculate the speed of a man who runs 70 m in 14 s.

2. How long will it take a man running at 10 m/s to travel 550 m?

3. Explain the difference between speed and velocity. Give one example of each.

4. Calculate the acceleration of an object which increases by 60 m/s in 20 s.

5. Calculate the final velocity of a car which, when travelling at 10 m/s, accelerates at 2 m/s^2 for 20 s.

6. Calculate the time it would take for an aircraft to increase its speed from rest to 100 m/s if its acceleration is 12.5 m/s^2.

Graphs of motion

It is often useful to show the *journey of an object* in the form of a graph.

There are two types of graph:

distance–time graphs and *speed– or velocity–time graphs*.

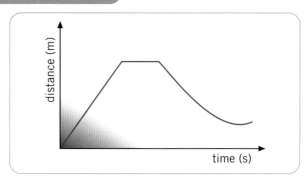

Distance–time graphs

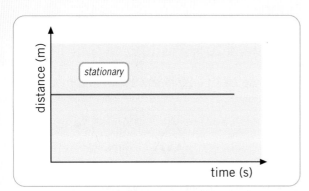

Horizontal line object is **not moving**.

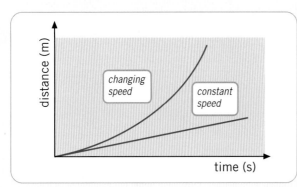

Steepness or gradient of line changes: speed of object is **not constant**.

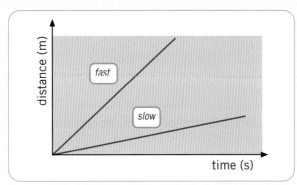

Sloping straight line: object moving at **constant speed**.

Steeper straight line: object moving at a **greater constant speed**.

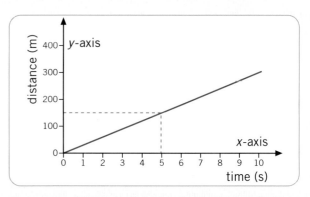

Speed of an object is equal to the **gradient of the line**.

$$\text{Speed of object} = \frac{y}{x} = \frac{150}{5} = 30 \text{ m/s}$$

Example

A bus moving at a constant speed travels 2000 m in 100 s. It then stops for 50 s to pick up passengers. Continuing its journey, the bus, again moving at a constant speed, travels 1000 m in the next 100 s.

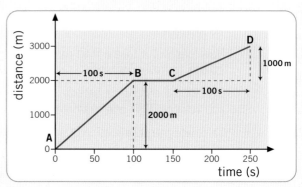

Speed– or velocity–time graphs

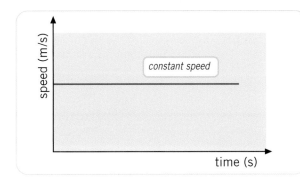

Horizontal line object moving at **constant speed**.

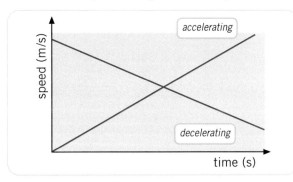

Line sloping upwards object increasing speed, i.e. **accelerating**.

Line sloping downwards: object decreasing speed, i.e. **decelerating**.

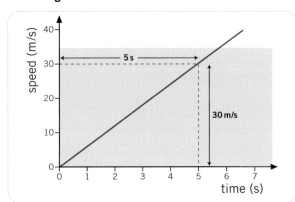

The **acceleration** of an object is equal to the **steepness** or **gradient** of its velocity–time graph.

Acceleration of car $= \dfrac{y}{x} = \dfrac{30}{5} = 6$ m/s per s (for 6 m/s^2)

Negative gradients indicate the object is **decelerating**.

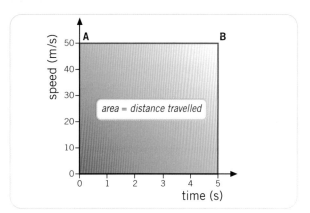

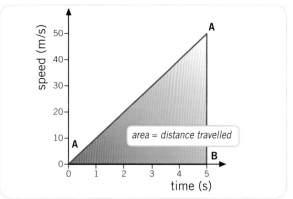

The **area** under a **speed–** or **velocity–time graph** shows the **distance** an object has travelled.

Example

A motorcyclist starting from rest accelerates to a speed of 40 m/s in 4 s. He travels at this speed for 10 s before decelerating to a halt in 8 s.

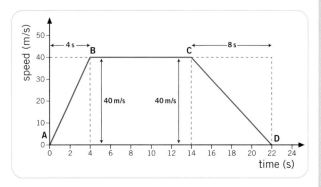

 If you have to draw a graph, remember to:
- *use a sharp pencil and don't press too hard. You may want to rub it out!*
- *use a ruler for straight lines and axes*
- *label the axes and include units.*

❶ On a distance–time graph what do the following show?
   a) a horizontal line
   b) a steeply sloping straight line
   c) a straight line sloping just a little.

❷ On a speed–time graph what do the following show?
   a) a horizontal line
   b) a straight line sloping steeply upwards
   c) a straight line sloping gently downwards.

Balanced and unbalanced forces

When two objects interact, the forces they exert
on each other are equal and opposite.

Forces and reaction

This television is
pushing down on its
stand with a force
which is equal to its
weight. The stand is
pushing upwards with
an equal force. This
force is often called
the **reaction**.

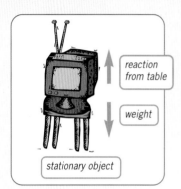

reaction
from table

weight

stationary object

This boy's
weight is applying a
force to the
branch. The branch
is applying an
equal and opposite
force to the boy.

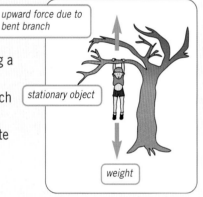

upward force due to
bent branch

stationary object

weight

If several forces are acting on an object, they can be
replaced by one force that has the same effect as all
the individual forces. This one force is called the
resultant force.

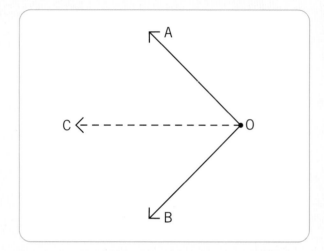

The two forces A and B acting on object O could be
replaced by one force (C) which has the same effect.
C is the resultant of A and B.

Balanced forces

If several forces are applied to an object, they may
cancel each other out. The resultant force is zero: the
forces are **balanced**.

The forces
applied to the
rope by both
teams are
balanced

balanced forces: no motion

If the forces applied to an object are **balanced**, they will
have **no effect on its motion**.

If the object is stationary, it will **remain stationary**. If
the object is moving, it will **continue to move in the same
direction** and at the **same speed**.

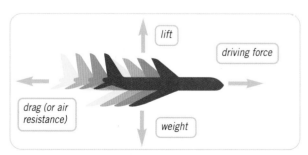

lift

driving force

drag (or air
resistance)

weight

If the driving force of this aircraft equals the drag, it
will travel at a constant speed. If the lift force equals
the weight, the aircraft will stay at a constant height.

Unbalanced forces

If the forces applied to an object do not cancel each other out, they are **unbalanced**. There is, therefore, a resultant force and this will affect the motion of the object.

unbalanced forces

If it is already moving it may:

■ stop moving
■ speed up
■ slow down
■ change direction.

stationary object made to move: unbalanced forces

If the object is stationary, it may start to move. It will move in the direction of the resultant force.

Forces and acceleration

An object whose motion is changing is accelerating. The size of the acceleration depends on:

■ The size of the force – the larger the force, the greater the acceleration.

■ The mass of the object – the larger the mass, the smaller the acceleration.

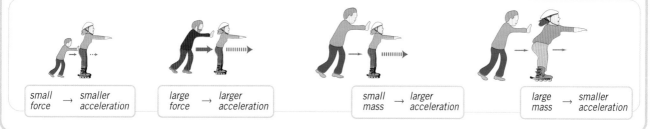

small force → smaller acceleration

large force → larger acceleration

small mass → larger acceleration

large mass → smaller acceleration

Calculating acceleration

When a force of F N is applied to an object of mass m kg, the resulting acceleration can be calculated using the equation:

Force = mass × acceleration (F = m × a)

We can write this as a formula triangle:

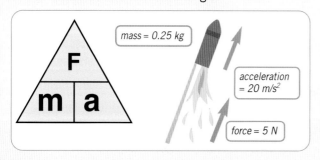

mass = 0.25 kg

acceleration = 20 m/s²

force = 5 N

Example

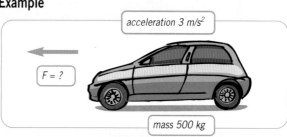

acceleration 3 m/s²

F = ?

mass 500 kg

Calculate the force required to give a car of mass 500 kg an acceleration of 3 m/s².

F = m × a = 500 kg × 3 m/s² = 1500 N or 1.5 kN.

💡 *Remember, balanced forces mean no change to speed or direction: unbalanced forces cause change.*

① What effect do balanced forces have on the motion of an object?

② What effect may unbalanced forces have on the motion of an object?

③ What does the size of the acceleration of an object depend upon?

④ Calculate the force needed to give an acceleration of 2 m/s² to a rock of mass 10 kg.

Frictional forces and terminal velocity

Whenever an object moves or tries to move, *friction* is present.

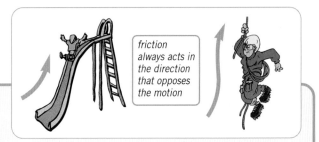

friction always acts in the direction that opposes the motion

Friction

flow of air around car

50 km/hr

driving force

friction

When an object moves through air or water, it will experience frictional or resistive forces, which will try to prevent its motion. This force is often called **drag**.

100 km/hr

driving force

friction

The faster the object moves, the larger these resistive forces become.

Terminal velocity: cars

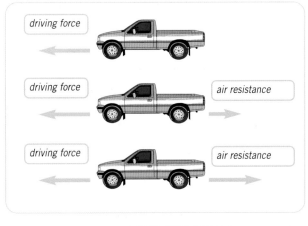

driving force

driving force · air resistance

driving force · air resistance

Action – the driver begins journey by pressing accelerator.

Result – the driving force from the engine creates a **resultant force**. The car accelerates in the direction of the resultant force.

Action – the accelerator is kept in the same position.

Result – as the speed of the car increases, the **air resistance** increases. The resultant force becomes smaller and so the car's acceleration is also smaller.

Action – the accelerator is kept in the same position.

Result – the air resistance and the driving force are equal and balanced. There is no resultant force. The car travels at a constant speed called its '**terminal velocity**'.

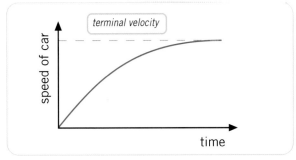

terminal velocity

speed of car

time

Terminal velocity: skydiving

Action	Result
Sky diver jumps from plane.	He accelerates downwards due to the force of gravity (weight).
Sky diver continues to fall.	His speed increases. His air resistance increases. So his acceleration decreases.
Still free-falling.	The air resistance and pull of gravity balance. He now falls at a constant speed called his terminal velocity.
Sky diver opens parachute.	His air resistance increases and he slows down.
Continues to fall with parachute open.	His speed continues to decrease until the air resistance and pull of gravity are balanced. He then falls at a much lower terminal velocity.
Sky diver lands on feet.	Ground provides an upward force bringing him to a halt.

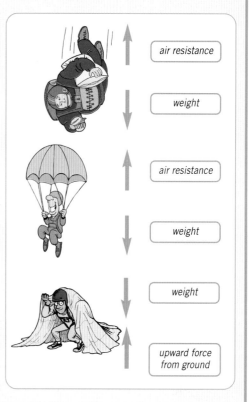

Try drawing and explaining the shape of the speed–time graph for a sky diver. If you can achieve this, you will really understand balanced forces and terminal velocity.

Weight

Acceleration due to gravity

The sky diver falls because he is in the Earth's gravitational field. This field (which we often call gravity) pulls all objects that have mass, downwards. The size of the force that does this is what we call the weight of the object. We can calculate the weight of an object using the following equation:

$$\text{weight} = \text{mass} \times \text{gravitational field strength}$$

or

$$w = m \times g$$

Example

Calculate the weight of a man whose mass is 80 kg. The Earth's gravitational field strength is 10 N/kg

$$W = m \times g = 80 \text{ kg} \times 10 \text{ N/kg} = 800 \text{ N}$$

QUICK TEST

1. What is friction?
2. In which direction does friction act?
3. What happens to a moving object if the driving force and the resistive forces are
   a) balanced?
   b) unbalanced, with the resultant force acting in the same direction as the resistive forces?
4. Suggest one way in which a sky diver could increase the terminal velocity he reaches before opening his parachute.
5. Calculate the weight of a woman whose mass is 65 kg.

Stopping distance

To avoid accidents, it is important that drivers can estimate the distance they need to bring a vehicle to a halt. Driving too close to the car in front is the cause of a large number of accidents, particularly on roads where the traffic is moving quickly, for example on motorways.

It's always important for a driver to know how quickly he can stop

Stopping a vehicle

In order to slow down or stop a vehicle, a **braking force** must be applied. This is often done by using the friction between surfaces.

The distance needed to bring a vehicle to a halt is called the **stopping distance**. It consists of two parts:

- the thinking distance – the distance a vehicle travels before a driver applies the brakes
- the braking distance – the distance the vehicle travels whilst braking.

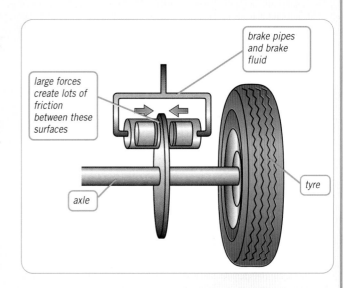

brake pipes and brake fluid

large forces create lots of friction between these surfaces

tyre

axle

Thinking distance

Factors that will affect the **thinking distance** are:
- **The speed of a vehicle** – the greater the speed, the greater the distance travelled before the brakes are applied.
- **The reaction time of the driver** – the slower a driver's reactions, the greater the distance travelled before

the brakes are applied. Drinking alcohol, taking drugs, tiredness and lack of concentration will all increase this time.
- Poor visibility may also delay the point at which a hazard is seen and the brakes applied.

Braking distance

STOPPING DISTANCES

Shortest stopping distances, on a dry road, with good brakes

At 13 m/s (30 miles/hour)

Thinking distance	Braking distance	Total stopping distance
9 m	14 m	23 m

23 m

At 22 m/s (50 miles/hour)

Thinking distance	Braking distance	Total stopping distance
15 m	38 m	53 m

53 m

At 30 m/s (70 miles/hour)

Thinking distance	Braking distance	Total stopping distance
21 m	75 m	96 m

96 m

☐ Thinking distance
☐ Stopping distance

Factors that will affect the **braking distance** are:

- **The mass of the vehicle** – the greater the mass, the greater the distance needed for it to come to a halt.
- **The speed of the vehicle** – speed affects the braking distance far more than most people realise. If a driver doubles his speed, he will need a braking distance that is at least four times longer.
- **The braking forces applied to the wheels** – faulty brakes can result in smaller forces being applied to the wheels, so increasing the braking distance. Drivers must also beware of applying too great a braking force, as the friction between the vehicle's tyres and the road surface may not be great enough to prevent skidding.

- **The frictional forces between the tyres and the road surface** – if these are reduced in any way, the braking distance will increase. Frictional forces will also be lessened:
  - by adverse weather conditions, such as wet or icy weather
  - if a car's tyres are worn and so provide poor grip
  - if the road surface is smooth.

🛈 *Remember, stopping distance = thinking distance + braking distance.*

🛈 *Knowledge of stopping distance is very important for road safety. Consequently, this is a very popular topic and well worth revising in detail.*

QUICK TEST

1. What is the 'thinking distance'?
2. What is the 'braking distance'?
3. What is the 'stopping distance'?
4. What kinds of forces are normally used in braking systems?
5. Explain how the following may affect a driver's thinking distance.
   a) the driver's age
   b) how many hours a driver has been driving
   c) the fact that the driver has not drunk alcohol or taken drugs
6. Explain how the following may affect the braking distance of a car.
   a) the mass of the car
   b) the speed of the car
   c) the condition of the car's tyres and the surface of the road
7. Look carefully at the stopping distances shown in this spread. Estimate
   a) the thinking distance
   b) the braking distance
   c) the total stopping distance for a car travelling at 26 m/s (60 m.p.h.)

Work and power

Work is done when a force is applied to an object and the object moves.

Power is the rate at which the work is being done.

Doing work

- **Work** is done when an **applied force moves an object**.
- This weightlifter is doing work.
- He is pushing these weights above his head.

To calculate the amount of work he has done we use the equation:

> work done = force × distance moved in direction of the force

> $W = F \times d$

In the above example:

> $W = 1000\ N \times 2.0\ m = 2000\ J$ or $2\ kJ$

- We measure work in **joules** (J) or **kilojoules** (kJ).
  1 kJ = 1000 J
- It may be useful to write the equation as a formula triangle:

Example

600 J of work are done when this lawnmower is pushed 10 m. Calculate the size of the force pushing the mower.

> Using $F = \dfrac{W}{d} = \dfrac{600\ J}{10\ m} = 60\ N$

Example

Whilst pushing this car with a force of 150 N, 60 kJ (i.e. 60 000 J) of work was done. How far was the car pushed?

> Using $d = \dfrac{W}{F} = \dfrac{60\ 000}{150} = 400\ m$

Remember that by using the formula triangle you should be able to calculate the work done or the time taken using the power equation.

Power

Power is the rate of doing work, i.e. how much work is done per second.

- We can calculate the power of a machine using the equation:

$$\text{power} = \frac{\text{work done}}{\text{time taken}} \quad \left(P = \frac{W}{t} \right)$$

- We measure power in **watts** (W) or **kilowatts** (kW).

Example

The power of this car engine is **1000 W**.

It can do **1000 J of work** in one second.

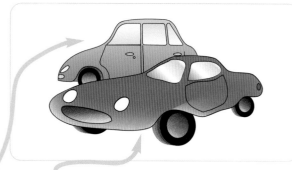

The power of this car engine is **3000 W**.

It is more powerful. Its engine can do **3000 J of work** every second.

Calculating power

Example

This crane is lifting a 10 000 N load to a height of 5 m.

$$W = F \times d = 10\ 000 \text{ N} \times 5 \text{ m} = 50\ 000 \text{ J or } 50 \text{ kJ}$$

If the crane can do this in 100 s, its power is:

$$P = \frac{W}{t} = \frac{50\ 000}{100} = 500 \text{ J/s or } 500 \text{ W}$$

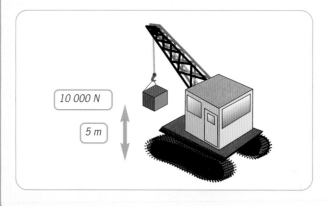

10 000 N

5 m

Example

This boy runs 10 m up a flight of stairs in just 5 s. He weighs 1200 N.

Calculate the work he does and his power.

$$W = F \times d = 600 \text{ N} \times 10 \text{ m} = 6\ 000 \text{ J or } 6 \text{ kJ}$$

Remember that the boy is doing work due to his vertical motion so it is the vertical distance he moves which is important.

$$P = \frac{W}{t} = \frac{6\ 000 \text{ J}}{5 \text{ s}} = 1\ 200 \text{ W or } 1.2 \text{ kW}$$

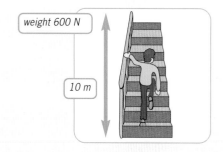

weight 600 N

10 m

QUICK TEST

1. Calculate the work done when a lawn roller is pushed 30 m by a force of 250 N.

2. Calculate the height to which a 500 N load is lifted by a crane if 20 kJ of work is done.

3. Calculate the force that is applied to a car engine if 1500 J of work is done when it is lifted onto a bench of height 1 m.

4. What is power?

5. Which units do we use to measure:
   a) work done?
   b) power?

6. Calculate the power of the person pushing the lawn roller in question 1 if the work is done in 25 s.

7. Calculate the power of the crane in question 2 if the lift takes 40 s.

Kinetic energy and potential energy

Kinetic energy

All moving objects possess **kinetic energy** (**KE**). The faster an object moves, the greater its kinetic energy; and the greater the mass of the object, the greater its kinetic energy. We can calculate how much kinetic energy an object has using the equation:

$$KE = \tfrac{1}{2}mv^2$$

Example

Calculate the kinetic energy of a cannon ball with a mass of 4 kg travelling at a speed of 40 m/s.

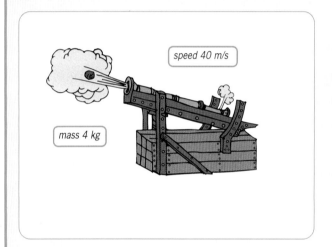

speed 40 m/s

mass 4 kg

$$KE = \tfrac{1}{2}mv^2 = \tfrac{1}{2} \times 4 \text{ kg} \times 1600 \text{ (m/s)}^2 = 3200 \text{ J}$$

Example

To bring a vehicle to a halt, **work** must be done by the frictional forces that equals the kinetic energy of the vehicle.

Calculate the work done in bringing a car with a mass of 500 kg, travelling at a speed of 30 m/s, to a halt.

mass 500 kg
speed 30 m/s

$$\text{Work done} = KE = \tfrac{1}{2}mv^2 = \tfrac{1}{2} \times 500 \text{ kg} \times 900 \text{ (m/s)}^2$$
$$= 225\,000 \text{ J or } 225 \text{ kJ}$$

Potential energy

Objects have **potential energy** because of their **position in the Earth's gravitational field**: the higher the object, the greater its potential energy; and the greater the mass of the object, the greater its potential energy. We can calculate the potential energy of an object using the equation:

$$PE = mgh$$

where g = the strength of the Earth's gravitational field.

Its value is 9.8 N/kg but an approximate value of 10 N/kg is often used.

Example

A man of mass 80 kg stands on the top of a building 20 m above the ground. Calculate his potential energy.

$$PE = mgh = 80 \text{ kg} \times 10 \text{ N/kg} \times 20 \text{ m}$$
$$= 16\,000 \text{ J or } 16 \text{ kJ}$$

The gravitational field strength on other planets or their moons is likely to be different from that of the Earth. This will, therefore, affect the potential energy of an object. The gravitational field strength on the Moon is approximately a sixth of that on the Earth. The man in the above example would only have a sixth of the potential energy if the building was on the Moon.

Energy transfers

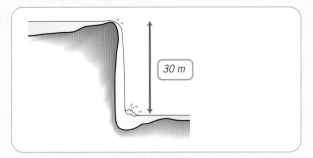

The water at the top of this waterfall has gravitational potential energy. As it falls, its potential energy is transferred into kinetic energy. At the bottom of the waterfall the kinetic energy gained by the water will equal the gravitational potential energy lost.

loss in potential energy = $mg\Delta h$
gain in kinetic energy = $\frac{1}{2}mv^2$

Therefore,

$$mg\Delta h = \frac{1}{2}mv^2$$
$$g\Delta h = \frac{1}{2}v^2$$

or

$$v = \sqrt{2 \times g\Delta h}$$
$$v = \sqrt{2 \times 10\ m/s^2 \times 30\ m}$$
$$v = 24.5\ m/s$$

The diagram opposite shows what happens when a ball is dropped on to a hard surface.

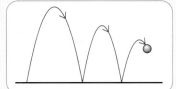

Each time the ball falls, its **potential energy is transferred into kinetic energy**.

Each time the ball rises, its **kinetic energy** is **transferred into potential energy**. If the transfer was 100% efficient,

the ball would always bounce back up to its original height. However, energy is lost during the bounce, as heat and sound. Energy is also lost as the ball moves through the air. As a result, the ball reaches a lower height after each bounce until it eventually stops. If, after each bounce, the ball only climbs to 75% of the previous height, the efficiency of the energy transfer is 75%.

At the start of the ride on this roller coaster the cars are pulled to the top of the first hill. This is the highest point on the track and so the cars have a lot of gravitational potential energy. When the cars are released they accelerate down the first slope, gaining speed as their potential energy is transferred into kinetic energy. As they climb the second slope, their kinetic energy is transferred back into potential energy, but because energy is lost they cannot climb as high. This loss of energy continues all the way around the track with the height of each hill climbed becoming less and less.

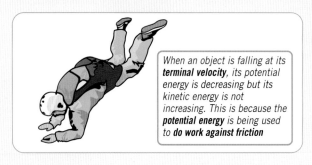

When an object is falling at its ***terminal velocity***, *its potential energy is decreasing but its kinetic energy is not increasing. This is because the* ***potential energy*** *is being used to* ***do work against friction***

QUICK TEST

1 What do we mean by the following phrases?
   a) kinetic energy
   b) potential energy

2 Calculate the kinetic energy of a model car that has a mass of 5 kg and is moving at a speed of 6 m/s.

3 Calculate the potential energy of a parcel with a mass of 10 kg that is placed on a shelf 3 m above the ground.

Momentum

As we have already seen, two important factors in determining the stopping distance of a car or lorry are its *mass* and its *velocity*. The larger the mass or the velocity, the more difficult it is to bring the vehicle to a halt quickly. We can describe these situations using the idea of *momentum*.

Calculating momentum

We can calculate the momentum of an object using the equation:

> **momentum = mass × velocity**

Example

Calculate the momentum of a car of mass 1000 kg moving with a velocity of 40 m/s.

> momentum = mass × velocity
> = 1000 kg × 40 m/s = 40 000 kg m/s

Example

Calculate the momentum of a lorry of mass 5000 kg moving with a velocity of 20 m/s.

> momentum = mass × velocity
> = 5000 kg × 20 m/s = 100 000 kg m/s

All moving objects have momentum. Momentum has size and direction. It is a **vector quantity**.

We can imagine momentum as being a measure of **how difficult it is to alter how an object is moving**.

Changing momentum 1

If we want to change the momentum of an object, make it travel faster or slower or change the direction in which it is moving, **we need to apply a force to it**. The size of this force depends upon:
- how big the change in momentum will be
- how quickly the change in momentum takes place.

It's easy to stop this.

If the change in momentum is small, only a small force needs to be applied to the object

It is much more difficult to stop this. It would need a very large force

If the change in momentum occurs slowly then only a small force needs to be applied

I only need to apply a small force. I'm in no hurry to stop him.

but

HELP!

The size of the force, and the change in the momentum of an object the force causes, are related by the equation:

$$\text{force} = \frac{\text{change in momentum}}{\text{time taken for the change}}$$

Changing momentum 2

Example

The momentum of a car changes by 2000 kg m/s in 5 s. Calculate the braking force applied to the car.

$$\text{force} = \frac{\text{change in momentum}}{\text{time taken for the change}}$$
$$= \frac{2000 \text{ kg m/s}}{5 \text{ s}} = 400 \text{ N}$$

Example

A car of mass 800 kg accelerates from rest to 50 m/s in 10 s.

Calculate the accelerating force applied to the car.

$$\text{momentum before} = 800 \text{ kg} \times 0 \text{ m/s} = 0 \text{ kg m/s}$$
$$\text{momentum after} = 800 \text{ kg} \times 50 \text{ m/s}$$
$$= 40\,000 \text{ kg m/s}$$
$$\text{change in momentum} = 40\,000 \text{ kg m/s} - 0 \text{ kg m/s}$$
$$= 40\,000 \text{ kg m/s}$$

$$\text{force} = \frac{\text{change in momentum}}{\text{time taken for the change}}$$
$$= \frac{40\,000 \text{ kg m/s}}{10 \text{ s}} = 4000 \text{ N}$$

Safety in cars

Momentum is an extremely important concept in car safety. Many injuries and fatalities are caused by the **large forces being applied to drivers and passengers during collisions**. The sizes of these forces would be much smaller, and the number of injuries and fatalities caused would be reduced, if the changes in momentum took place over a longer period of time.

Crumple zones

During a collision, most modern cars are now designed so that part of the car body, known as the **crumple zone**, gradually crumples. This **increases the time during which the momentum is changing** and so **reduces the forces** applied to the driver and passengers.

Seat belts

Seat belts are designed to **stretch slightly**. During a collision, this stretching increases the time during which a person's momentum changes and so reduces the forces being applied to a much safer level.

QUICK TEST

1. Explain what is meant by the 'momentum of an object'.

2. Calculate the momentum of a motorcycle of mass 150 kg when it is travelling at 60 m/s.

3. Calculate the braking force required to change the momentum of a lorry by 10 000 kg m/s in 5 s.

4. Explain why cars with crumple zones are safer during collisions than cars that have no crumple zones.

5. Why do air bags reduce injuries and fatalities in car collisions?

Collisions and explosions

When objects collide, their *velocities will change*. As a result, the *momentum* of each object will also change.

Collisions

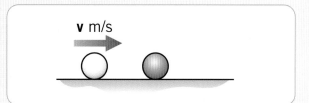

When the white snooker ball hits the red ball, the momentum of each ball will change. There are several possible results:
- After the **collision**, the white ball will be **stationary** and the red ball will move.
- After the collision, the white ball and the red ball will both move in the same direction.
- After the collision, the white ball moves back in the direction from which it came and the red ball moves away in the opposite direction.

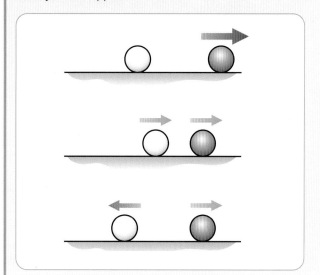

All three of these outcomes are possible and they all share one common feature. The **total momentum of the two balls before the collision must equal the total momentum of the balls after the collision.**

Interactions between objects like this are described by the **Principle of Conservation of Momentum**, which states:

> When two or more bodies act on each other, their total momentum remains constant, providing there is no external force acting.

Example
A ball of mass 0.2 kg, travelling at 6 m/s, strikes a stationary second ball of mass 0.15 kg. Calculate the velocity of the second ball if, after the collision, the first ball continues to move in the same direction at 1.5 m/s.

$$\text{total momentum before} = \text{total momentum after}$$
$$0.2 \text{ kg} \times 6 \text{ m/s} + 0.15 \text{ kg} \times 0 \text{ m/s}$$
$$= 0.2 \text{ kg} \times 1.5 \text{ m/s} + 0.15 \text{ kg} \times v$$
$$1.2 \text{ kg m/s} - 0.3 \text{ kg m/s} = 0.15 \text{ kg} \times v$$
$$v = 6 \text{ m/s}$$

Example
A bullet of mass 0.02 kg enters a stationary block of wood at 400 m/s. Calculate the speed of the block of wood immediately after impact if there are no frictional forces and the mass of the block is 0.48 kg.

$$\text{total momentum before} = \text{total momentum after}$$
$$0.02 \text{ kg} \times 400 \text{ m/s} + 0.48 \text{ kg} \times 0 \text{ m/s}$$
$$= (0.02 \text{ kg} + 0.48 \text{ kg}) \times v$$
$$v = \frac{8.00 \text{ kg m/s}}{0.50 \text{ kg}} = 16 \text{ m/s}$$

Explosions

The Principle of Conservation of Momentum applies to **explosions** as well as collisions.

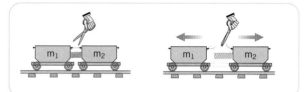

When the thread holding these two wagons together is cut, they will move away from each other in the same way that particles in an explosion move away from each other.

Before the thread is cut, the total momentum of the bodies is zero. As the wagons move apart, if there are no external forces acting, the total momentum must still be zero.

total momentum before = total momentum after

$$0 = m_1 \times v_1 - m_2 \times v_2$$

The minus sign shows that one wagon is moving in the opposite direction to the other wagon.

$$m_1 \times v_1 = m_2 \times v_2$$

Rockets

Rockets use a kind of **controlled explosion** to **propel themselves forward**. Hot gases are pushed out of the back of the rocket. The rocket itself then gains a momentum equal to that of the **ejected gases**, but in the opposite direction.

Example

From the information given in the diagram below, calculate the velocity of wagon B.

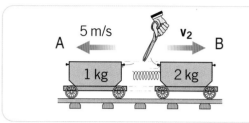

$$m_1 \times v_1 = m_2 \times v_2$$
$$1 \text{ kg} \times 5 \text{ m/s} = 2 \text{ kg} \times v_2$$
$$v_2 = 2.5 \text{ m/s}$$

When the trigger is pulled during clay pigeon shooting, the shot is ejected at great speed from the barrel, whilst the gun moves in the opposite direction. This reaction to the ejecting of the shot is called the **recoil**.

Example

Calculate the recoil velocity of a shotgun given the following information:

mass of shot = 0.3 kg
velocity of shot = 200 m/s
mass of gun = 3.0 kg

$$m_1 \times v_1 = m_2 \times v_2$$
$$0.3 \text{ kg} \times 200 \text{ m/s} = 3.0 \text{ kg} \times v_2$$
$$v_2 = 20 \text{ m/s}$$

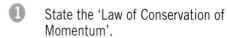

QUICK TEST

1. State the 'Law of Conservation of Momentum'.

2. A box of mass 4 kg travelling at 5 m/s strikes a second box, also of mass 4 kg. Calculate the velocity of the second box if the first box stops after the collision. You can assume that external forces, such as friction, are negligible.

3. A dart of mass 100 g (0.1 kg), moving with a velocity of 50 m/s, is shot into a piece of wood of mass 0.9 kg. Calculate the initial velocity of the dart and wood immediately after impact.

4. Calculate the recoil velocity of a cannon given the following information.
mass of cannon ball = 10 kg
velocity of shot = 100 m/s
mass of gun = 200 kg

Motion in a circle

If an object is moving in a *circle* there is a force acting on it. The direction of the force is towards the centre of the circle.

The thrill of rides like the one shown is experiencing the force needed to travel in a circle.

Accelerating at a constant speed

If a moving object is not accelerating, it:
■ is travelling in a straight line
■ is travelling at a constant speed
■ has no resultant force acting upon it.

If an object is travelling in a circle it may be travelling at a constant speed, but its direction is continually changing. This means that it is accelerating and that there must be a force acting on it. This force is called a **centripetal force**.

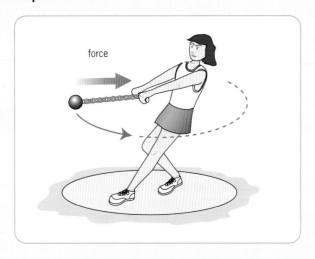

As the girl in the diagram below spins around she makes the ball at the end of the rope travel in a circle. To do this, she must pull on the rope. She is applying a force to the ball. The direction of this force is towards the centre of the circle that it is travelling around.

The diagram above shows what would happen if the rope snapped or the girl released the rope. A force is no longer being applied to the ball and so it stops changing direction and moves off in a straight line.

All objects moving in a circle are experiencing a force that is making them change direction.

Using and experiencing centripetal forces

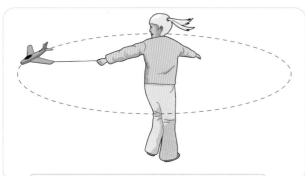

As long as the controller continues to pull on the wire, the model aircraft will continue to travel in a circle

The forces applied to you when you travel in a vertical circle can be even more exciting

During take off, astronauts experience very large forces, often call **g-forces**. This machine, called a centrifuge, is used to train the astronauts to withstand these forces. The astronaut sits inside the capsule at the end of the arm. The arm then rotates moving the astronaut in a circle. The faster the **centrifuge** spins around, the greater the forces applied to the astronaut.

The faster an object moves around a circle, the greater the force that must be applied to it. This bobsleigh and the team inside it are experiencing very large forces as they travel through curves at very high speeds. It is forces similar to these (but much lower) that we find so exciting on many fairground rides.

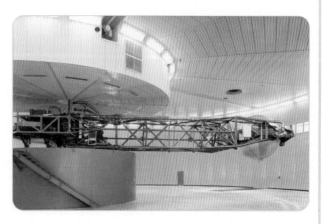

1. Describe the motion of an object that is not accelerating.

2. What resultant force is acting on an object that is not accelerating?

3. How do we know that an object travelling in a circle is accelerating?

4. Describe the force acting on an object that is travelling in a circle. What happens to the size of this force if the object increases its speed?

Static electricity

Did you know that lightning is caused by static electricity? Where do the charges come from?

Atoms contain *positively charged particles* called *protons*. They also contain *negatively charged particles* called *electrons*. *Neutral atoms* have *equal numbers* of *protons* and electrons.

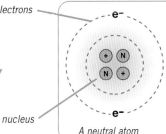

A neutral atom

orbiting electrons

nucleus

+ positively charged proton

N uncharged particle (neutron)

e- negatively charged electron

How do we make static electricity?

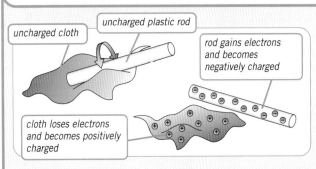

uncharged cloth

uncharged plastic rod

rod gains electrons and becomes negatively charged

cloth loses electrons and becomes positively charged

■ Electrons belonging to one object can sometimes be transferred to another object simply by rubbing them together.

■ Both objects should be **insulators**, that is made from, for example, plastic and cloth. Neither of them should be **conductors**, that is, made from a metal.

■ Insulators **do not allow** charges to pass through them.

■ Conductors **allow** charges to pass through them easily.

■ As the insulators are rubbed together, one of them **gains electrons** and becomes **negatively charged**.

■ The other **loses electrons** and becomes **positively charged**.

Forces between charges

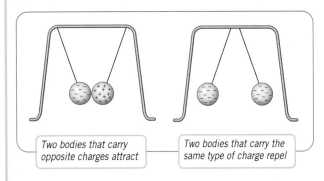

Two bodies that carry opposite charges attract

Two bodies that carry the same type of charge repel

Voltage, sparks and earthing

As the amount of charge on an **object** increases, the **repulsion** between charges also increases. As a result, **potential difference between the body and the earth increases**. If the potential difference becomes large enough, the charges may jump gaps in order to reach earth and escape. The body has **discharged**. If this happens, you may hear and see a spark.

Sparking can be dangerous. When liquids flow quickly through pipes they may become charged in the same way that two bodies become charged when they are

rubbed together. If a liquid is inflammable, such as petrol and aviation fuel, there is the danger that a spark may cause an explosion. To prevent this from happening when aeroplanes are being refuelled, the tankers and planes are connected together by a conductor before refuelling begins.

If the potential difference between the two spheres is high enough, sparking will occur as charges jump the gap in the air and escape to earth

Whilst you are travelling in a car you may become charged. When you step out of the car the charges will try to escape to earth. Sometimes you can be the route to earth!

Uses of static electricity

Electrostatic spraying

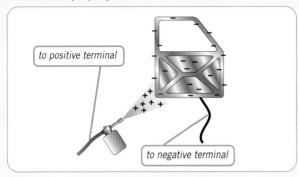

to positive terminal

to negative terminal

- The nozzle of the spray is connected to a **positive terminal**.
- The paint droplets become **positively charged** as they emerge from the nozzle.
- **Repulsion** between the **similarly charged droplets** keeps the paint as a **fine spray**.
- The object to be painted is connected to a **negative terminal**.
- The paint is attracted to the **oppositely charged object**. As a result, less paint is wasted and really awkward spots still get a good coat of paint.

Removing dust from smoke

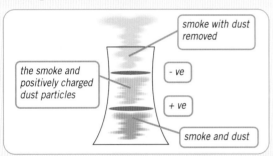

smoke with dust removed

the smoke and positively charged dust particles

- ve

+ ve

smoke and dust

- As the dust particles (ash) pass through the first set of plates, they become **positively charged**.
- As they pass through the second set, they are **attracted by the opposite charge**.
- The ash sticks to the negative plates.

- The cleaner smoke continues up the chimney.
- Every so often, the plates are shaken to remove the ash.

Photocopiers
- The surface of a rotating drum is charged.
- A bright light is shone on the page to be copied.
- The light parts of the paper reflect light onto the drum: the dark parts do not.
- The drum loses charge from those parts of the surface that have received the reflected light.
- Fine charged powder, called toner, is blown across the drum. It sticks only to those parts that are still charged.
- A sheet of paper is pressed against the drum and picks up the pattern of the carbon powder.
- The powder is fixed in place by a heater.

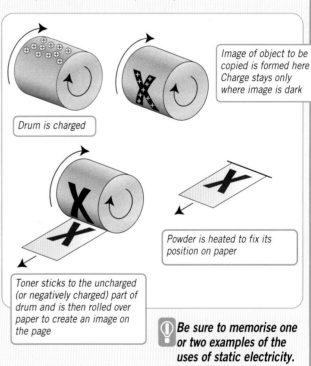

Drum is charged

Image of object to be copied is formed here Charge stays only where image is dark

Powder is heated to fix its position on paper

Toner sticks to the uncharged (or negatively charged) part of drum and is then rolled over paper to create an image on the page

Be sure to memorise one or two examples of the uses of static electricity.

---

1. What are the names of the charged particles in an atom?
2. How many of these charged particles are there in a neutral atom?
3. Which particles move when an object becomes charged?
4. Explain the difference between a conductor and an insulator.
5. Give one use of static electricity.
6. Give one disadvantage of static electricity.

Circuits, currents and resistance

An electric *current* is *a flow of charge*.

In metals, the charges are normally carried *by electrons*. Metals are *good conductors* because they contain lots of electrons that *are able to move around easily*.

Non-metals are usually *poor conductors or insulators*, because *they do not allow charges to move through them easily*.

In liquids, charges are carried by charged particles called *ions*. The process of sending a current through a liquid is called *electrolysis*.

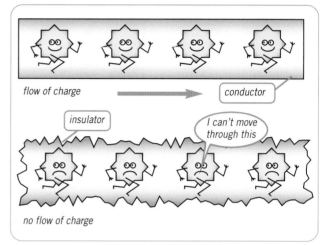

flow of charge   conductor

insulator   I can't move through this

no flow of charge

Making charges flow

Cells and batteries act as **charge pumps**, giving the charges **energy**. Several cells connected together can give more energy to the charges and produce a larger current in the circuit. Several cells connected together are called a **battery**.

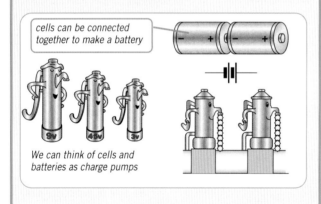

cells can be connected together to make a battery

We can think of cells and batteries as charge pumps

Circuits

Currents flow around **complete circuits**.

Current will not flow around a circuit if it is an **incomplete circuit**.

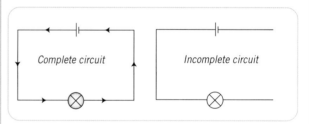

Complete circuit   Incomplete circuit

There are two types of circuit: **series circuits** and **parallel circuits**.

Parallel circuits

- Parallel circuits have **branches** and **junctions**.
- There is **more than one path** for the current to follow: there is choice.
- Switches can be put into the circuit to turn on and off all, or just part, of the circuit.
- The size of currents flowing in different parts of the circuit may be different.

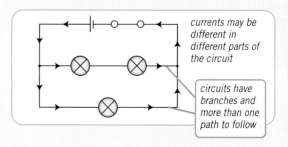

currents may be different in different parts of the circuit

circuits have branches and more than one path to follow

Series circuits

- Series circuits have **no branches** or junctions.
- There is only one path for the current to follow.
- The **same current** passes through **all parts** of the circuit.

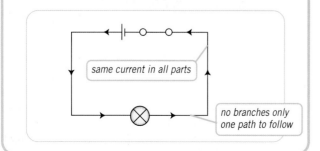

same current in all parts

no branches only one path to follow

Resistance

Components in a circuit **resist current** flowing through them.

- If a **small current** flows when a **large potential difference (voltage)** is applied across a component, the component has a **high resistance**.
- If a **large current** flows when a **small potential difference** is applied across a component, that component has a **low resistance**.

We **measure the resistance** of a component in **ohms (Ω)**. If a potential difference of 1 V causes a current of 1 A to flow through a component, it has a resistance of 1 Ω.

We can write this statement as a formula.

$$V = I \times R$$

Using the formula triangle, we can use this equation in several different forms.

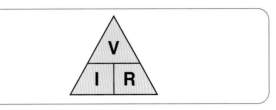

Example

A current of 3 A flows when a potential difference of 12 V is applied across a wire. Calculate the resistance of the wire.

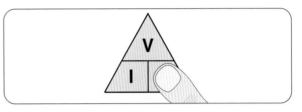

$$R = \frac{V}{I} = \frac{12\ V}{3\ A} = 4\ \Omega$$

Special resistors you need to know about

Light-dependent resistors (LDRs)

Light-dependent resistors have a **high resistance** when there is **little or no light**. Their **resistance decreases** as **light intensity increases**. They are used in **light-sensitive circuits**: for example, to control streetlighting, in burglar alarms and in digital cameras, to control the length of time that light is allowed to pass through the lens.

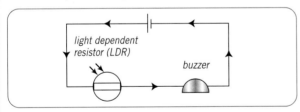

Thermistors

Thermistors are resistors whose **resistance alters as their temperature changes**. Most thermistors have **resistances that decrease** as their **temperature increases**. They are used in **temperature-sensitive circuits**: for example, in fire alarms and thermostats.

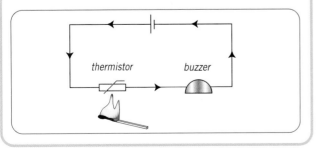

Using resistors

We can use **resistors** to **control the size of the current** flowing in a circuit.

If a **variable resistor** is included in a circuit, its value can be altered so that the current flowing in a circuit can be easily changed.

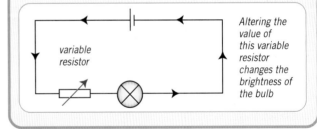

Altering the value of this variable resistor changes the brightness of the bulb

variable resistor

1. What is an electric current?
2. What are the particles which carry charges:
   a) in metals?
   b) in liquids?
3. What is a battery?
4. What is a circuit without gaps called?
5. In which type of circuit:
   a) is the current the same everywhere?
   b) are there branches or junctions?
6. In what units do we measure resistance?
7. Give one use for a light-dependent resistor.
8. Calculate the resistance of a fixed resistor which has a current of 2 A flowing through it when a voltage of 9 V is applied across its ends.

Domestic electricity

The electricity we use in the home is known as *mains electricity*. It is generated at a power station and transmitted to us through the *National Grid*. It is different from the electricity we use from cells and batteries in several ways.

a.c./d.c.

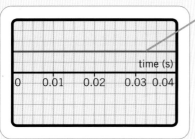

CRO shows type of current and voltage

horizontal line shows current/voltage has a steady value and passes in one direction. This is a DC current from a cell or battery

time (s)

0   0.01   0.02   0.03 0.04

the electricity we get from the mains

wave-shaped line shows an AC current/voltage which is continuously changing direction. The frequency of the supply $(f) = \frac{1}{T} = \frac{1}{0.02} = 50$ Hz.

time (s)

0   0.01   0.02   0.03 0.04

T

The electricity we get from cells and batteries is **one-way electricity**. It is called **direct current (d.c.)**. The electricity from the mains is **continuously changing**

direction: it is **alternating current (a.c.)**. It **flows back and forth 50 times every second**, that is, it has a **frequency of 50 Hz**.

The 3-pin plug

The voltage of the electricity from cells and batteries is quite low, for example 9 V or 12 V.

The voltage from the mains is about 230 V. It can **be dangerous if not used safely. Most appliances** are, therefore, **connected** to the mains using **insulated plugs**.

It is very important that the wires in a plug are connected to the **correct pins**. Looking at an open plug, like the one shown above, you will see that the **BRown** wire goes to the **Bottom Right** and that the **BLue** wire goes to the **Bottom Left**. The green and yellow wire (earth) goes to the pin at the top.

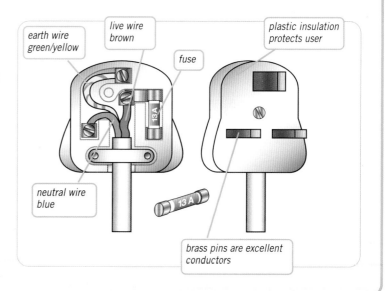

earth wire green/yellow

live wire brown

fuse

plastic insulation protects user

neutral wire blue

brass pins are excellent conductors

13 A

Fuses 1

All 3-pin plugs in the UK contain a **fuse**. This usually consists of a small **cylinder or cartridge** containing a thin piece of **wire with a low melting point**.

If a fault develops in a circuit and **too much current**

passes through the fuse, the **wire will melt**. The circuit becomes **incomplete** and **current ceases to pass through it**. The fuse **protects the user** and **limits any damage** to the electrical appliance.

Fuses 2

Fuses are given a **rating**, which indicates the **maximum current** that can flow through it without it melting. The most common fuses in the UK have ratings of 1 A, 3 A, 5 A and 13 A.

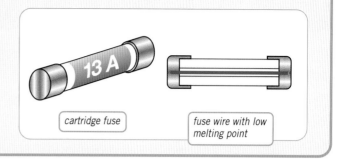

cartridge fuse

fuse wire with low melting point

Circuit-breakers

Circuit-breakers are a **special kind of fuse** that cause a break in a circuit if too much current flows through the circuit. Once the fault has been put right, the fuse is **usually reset by pushing a button**.

Residual circuit-breakers, like the one seen here, are often used when mowing the lawn or using hedge trimmers. They will detect current flowing to earth if a cable is cut. The instant this happens, the supply is turned off so that the user comes to no harm.

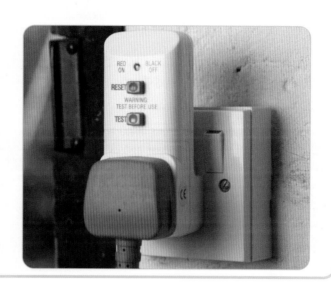

The earth wire

A 3-pin plug usually has three wires connected to it. The **electrical energy** travels into an appliance **through the live wire**. The supply alternates between positive and negative potentials. The **neutral wire** is the **return path** for the current and is kept at a potential close to zero. The **earth wire** is a safety connection which **protects the user** if an appliance becomes faulty.

If a kettle has a metal casing and the heating element is broken, anyone touching the casing will receive **an electric shock**. With the **earth wire connected**, the user is safe and will not receive an electric shock.

This **current blows the fuse, protecting the user**. Modern appliances, such as kettles, now have **plastic casings** to further reduce the risk of an electric shock for the user. The kettle in this diagram has **double insulation**.

1. What kind of current is supplied by the domestic mains?

2. In a typical domestic plug, what colour is a) the live wire b) the earth wire and c) the neutral wire?

3. Why are the pins of the domestic plug made from brass?

4. Name one advantage a circuit-breaker has over a cylinder fuse.

5. Give two situations when a residual circuit breaker might be used.

Electrical power

All *electrical appliances transfer electrical energy* into *other forms*.

This *hairdryer* transfers *electrical energy* into *heat and kinetic* and some *sound energy*.

This *radio* changes *electrical energy* into *sound energy*.

The *power* of an appliance is a measure of how quickly these energy *changes take place*. This *power rating* is *measured in watts (W)*.

The meaning of power

If a light bulb has a **power rating of 40 W**, it transfers **40 J of electrical energy** into heat and light energy **every second**.

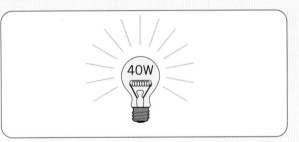

If an electrical fire has a **power rating of 2 kW** (2000 W), it **transfers 2000 J of electrical energy** into 2000 J of heat and light energy **every second**.

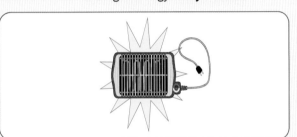

How many joules of energy have been transferred?

To calculate the total amount of energy an appliance has transferred we use the equation:

Energy = Power × time (in seconds)

or

E = P × t

This can be written as a formula triangle.

Example

How much electrical energy is transferred into heat and light energy when a 60 W bulb is turned on for 5 minutes?

E = P x t = 60 W × 300 s = 18 000 J or 18 kJ

Example

What is the power of a heater that transforms 120 kJ of electrical energy into heat energy in one minute?

$$P = \frac{E}{t} = \frac{120\ 000\ J}{60\ s} = 2000\ W\ (2\ kW)$$

Example

How long must a 100 W radio be turned on to transfer 3000 J of electrical energy into other forms of energy?

$$t = \frac{E}{P} = \frac{3000\ J}{100\ W} = 30\ s$$

The rate at which energy is transformed in a device is called its 'power'.

Power, potential difference and current

If we know the potential difference across an electrical device and the current flowing through it, we can calculate its power using the equation:

> **Power (W) = current (A) × potential difference (V)**

or

> **P = I × V**

This can be written as a formula triangle.

$$\frac{P}{I \mid V}$$

Example

When the potential difference applied across an electric heater is 230 V, a current of 12.5 A flows. Calculate the power of the heater.

> $P = V \times I = 230\ V \times 12.5\ A = 2875\ W$ or $2.875\ kW$

Which fuse?

Choosing the correct value of fuse for a circuit is important. If the fuse selected has too low a rating, it will melt (blow) and turn off the circuit, even when there is no fault and the correct current is flowing. If the fuse has too high a rating it will not protect the circuit and user when too large a current flows. The correct value of fuse is one that is **just large enough to allow the correct current to flow**: for example, if the usual current is 2 A, a 3 A fuse should be selected.

Calculating the correct value

If we know the **power rating of an appliance** connected to the mains supply, we can calculate the value of the fuse that should be used in the circuit using the equation:

> $$I = \frac{P}{V}$$

Example

Calculate the correct fuse needed for a heater rated at **230 V** 2 kW.

> $$I = \frac{P}{V} = \frac{2000}{230} = 8.7\ A$$

The correct fuse would, therefore, be a 13 A fuse.

💡 *Draw the equations **E = P × t** and **P = I × V** as formula triangles. When you have done that, try practising some problems. Questions using these equations are very popular with examiners.*

---

❶ How many joules of electrical energy are transferred into other forms when these appliances are turned on for one minute (60 seconds)?
   a) 100 W bulb
   b) 500 W computer and monitor
   c) 600 W hairdryer
   d) 1000 W heater
   e) 2 kW tumble dryer

❷ What is the power of a bulb that transfers 1200 J of electrical energy into heat and light energy in one minute?

❸ When the potential difference applied across an electric iron is 230 V, a current of 3 A flows. Calculate the power of the electric iron.

❹ Calculate the correct fuse needed for a radio rated at 230 V 500 W.

The structure of atoms

For many years, scientists thought that atoms were the smallest particles that could exist.

With a greater understanding of electricity it was suggested that atoms must contain positive and negative charges.

A scientist called J J Thomson suggested that atoms have a positive body which contains negative particles, like a pudding which contains plums.

An experiment was carried out by two scientists called Johannes Wilhelm Geiger and Ernst Marsden, supervised by Ernest Rutherford. They suggested a different model which was rapidly accepted as being correct.

The experiment they carried out was called the *alpha-particle scattering experiment*.

The alpha-particle scattering experiment

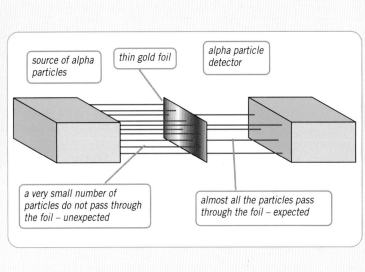

source of alpha particles

thin gold foil

alpha particle detector

a very small number of particles do not pass through the foil – unexpected

almost all the particles pass through the foil – expected

- Small particles called **alpha particles** were 'shot' at a **very thin piece of gold foil**.
- Most of the particles **passed straight through the foil** and were undeviated.
- This suggests that most of an atom is **empty space**.
- Some particles were deviated a little.
- A very small number **travelled back** almost in the direction from which they came.
- This suggests that most of the mass of an atom is concentrated in a **very small central nucleus** and that this centre must be positively charged.
- The model became known as the **nuclear atom**.

The nuclear atom

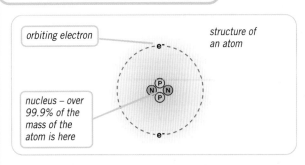

orbiting electron

structure of an atom

nucleus – over 99.9% of the mass of the atom is here

- Neutrons have a **relative atomic mass of 1**, but carry **no charge**.
- **Orbiting the nucleus** at very high speeds are extremely small particles called electrons.
- Electrons have a **very small mass** (about one two-thousandth of a proton) and carry a charge of **−1**.

- An atom has a **central core** called **the nucleus** which contains nearly **all the mass** of the atom.
- Within the nucleus are two types of particles: **protons** and **neutrons**.
- Protons have a **relative atomic mass of 1** and carry a charge of **+1**.

Particle	Place	Relative mass	Relative charge
Proton	In nucleus	1	+1
Neutron	In nucleus	1	0
Electron	In orbit around nucleus	$0(\frac{1}{2000})$	−1

Important facts about atoms

■ Atoms have **no overall charge**. They are **neutral**.
■ They must therefore **contain equal numbers of protons and electrons**.
■ The number of protons an atom has in its nucleus is called the **proton number**, or the **atomic number**.

■ The number of protons + the number of neutrons an atom has in its nucleus is called the **nucleon number** or the **mass number**.

The periodic table

There are over 100 different **elements**. Information about their **atomic structure** is contained in the **Periodic Table**.

The upper number is the element's nucleon number.
The lower number is the element's proton number.

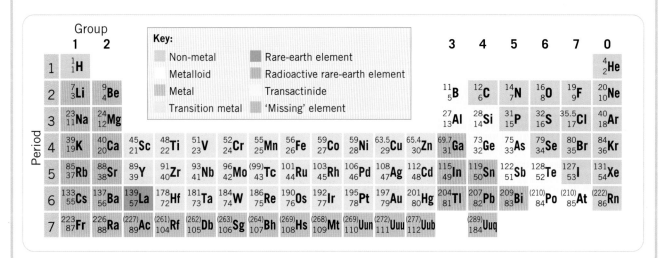

QUICK TEST

1. What was the name of the model of the atom suggested by Geiger and Marsden's experiment?

2. Where are the neutrons in an atom?

3. What charge is carried by an electron?

4. How many electrons and protons are there in a neutral atom?

5. Using the Periodic Table, find out the proton number of oxygen and the nucleon number of nitrogen.

Nuclear radiations

The *nuclei* of some atoms are *unstable*. As a result they constantly give out *radiation* in order to become more stable. These substances are said to be *radioactive*. There are three types of radiation that might be emitted. These are called *alpha*, *beta* and *gamma* radiation.

These nuclear radiations can be very useful, but they can also be very dangerous.

Absorption of any of the three types of radiation by living cells is potentially dangerous. It may cause *cell damage* and lead to illnesses such as *cancer*. Higher levels of exposure to these radiations may even *kill living cells*. It is, therefore, important that we understand their properties.

Alpha radiation (α)

Alpha particles are **slow-moving helium nuclei**, that is, they consist of **two protons and two neutrons**.

They are **big and heavy** and so have **poor penetrating power** (just a few centimetres in air).

They collide with lots of atoms **knocking some of their electrons off** and **creating ions**. They are **very good ionisers**.

An **ion** is an atom that has become charged by either losing or gaining electrons.

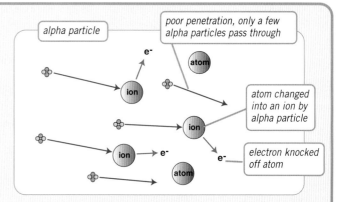

alpha particle

poor penetration, only a few alpha particles pass through

atom changed into an ion by alpha particle

electron knocked off atom

They are **positively charged** and so can be **deflected by electric and magnetic fields**.

Beta radiation (β)

These are **fast moving electrons**.

They are small and so possess **quite good powers of penetration**, up to about a metre in air.

They do collide with atoms and produce ions but not as many as the alpha particles.

They are **negatively charged** and so can be **deflected by electric and magnetic fields**.

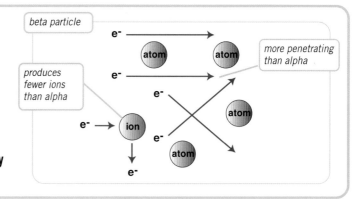

beta particle

more penetrating than alpha

produces fewer ions than alpha

Gamma rays (γ)

Gamma rays are **short-wavelength electromagnetic waves**, similar to X-rays.

They **travel at the speed of light** and are **very penetrating**. They can travel almost unlimited distances through the air.

They do not hit many atoms as they travel through a material and so are **very poor ionisers**.

Gamma radiation **carries no charge** and so is **unaffected by magnetic and electric fields**.

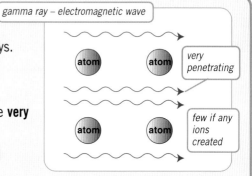

gamma ray – electromagnetic wave

very penetrating

few if any ions created

Comparison of the properties of alpha, beta and gamma radiation

Radiation	α	β	γ
Mass	4	negligible ($\frac{1}{2000}$)	0
Charge	+2	−1	0
Relative ionising power	100 000	1000	1
Approximate penetrating power in air	1–5 cm	10–80 cm	almost unlimited

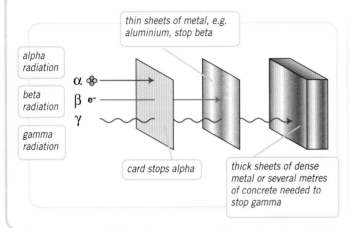

alpha radiation
beta radiation
gamma radiation

α ⊕
β e⁻
γ

thin sheets of metal, e.g. aluminium, stop beta

card stops alpha

thick sheets of dense metal or several metres of concrete needed to stop gamma

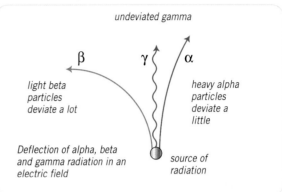

undeviated gamma

β   γ   α

light beta particles deviate a lot

heavy alpha particles deviate a little

Deflection of alpha, beta and gamma radiation in an electric field

source of radiation

Sources of radioactivity

There are radioactive substances all around us. Some are manmade and are used in hospitals, nuclear power stations and even in the home. Most of the radioactive substances around us occur naturally. They are in the ground, in the food we eat, and even in the air we breathe. Some radiation reaches us from space.

The radiation produced by these sources is called **background radiation**.

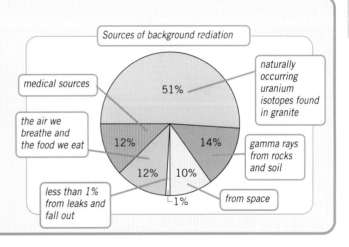

Sources of background radiation

medical sources

the air we breathe and the food we eat

less than 1% from leaks and fall out

51%

12%

12%

10%

1%

14%

naturally occurring uranium isotopes found in granite

gamma rays from rocks and soil

from space

 Name two effects exposure to radiation may have on living cells.

 Why do some nuclei give out radiation?

❸ Why is it important that we understand the properties of alpha, beta and gamma radiation?

 Which type of radiation is:
a) the most penetrating?
b) the best ioniser?
c) negatively charged?
d) a fast moving electron?
e) an electromagnetic wave?

Radioactive decay

The emission of alpha, beta or gamma radiation from a nucleus is called *radioactive decay*.

Radioactive decay equations

Alpha emission

An unstable nucleus changes into a stable nucleus by emitting an alpha particle.

$$^{226}_{88}\text{Ra} \longrightarrow ^{222}_{86}\text{Rn} + ^{4}_{2}\text{He}$$

| unstable radium nucleus | more stable radon nucleus | emitted alpha particle |

Beta emission

An unstable nucleus changes into a more stable nucleus by emitting a beta particle.

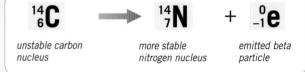

$$^{14}_{6}\text{C} \longrightarrow ^{14}_{7}\text{N} + ^{0}_{-1}\text{e}$$

| unstable carbon nucleus | more stable nitrogen nucleus | emitted beta particle |

Gamma emission

After an unstable nucleus has emitted an alpha or beta particle, it sometimes has a surplus of energy. It gets rid of this excess energy by emitting gamma radiation.

$$^{238}_{92}\text{U} \longrightarrow ^{234}_{90}\text{Th} + ^{4}_{2}\text{He} + ^{0}_{0}\gamma$$

| unstable uranium nucleus | more stable nitrogen nucleus | emitted alpha particle | emitted excess energy– gamma radiation |

Half-life

The **amount of radiation emitted each second** (the **activity of a source**) depends upon **how many unstable nuclei are present**. As time goes by, the **number of unstable nuclei** in a sample **decreases**. Therefore, the **activity of a source decreases with time**. We describe this decrease using the idea of a **half-life**.

The half-life of a radioactive material is the average time it takes for the number of undecayed nuclei in a sample of material to halve.

Different radioactive materials have different half-lives.

Isotope	Half-life
uranium-238	4500 million years
radium-226	1620 years
strontium-90	28 days
radon-222	4 days
radium-214	20 minutes

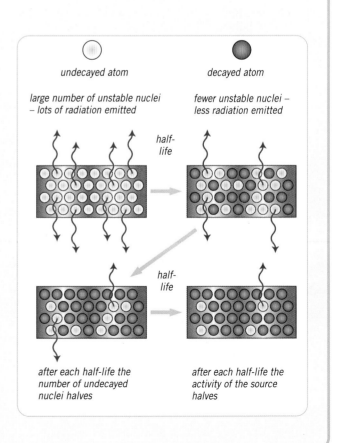

undecayed atom   decayed atom

large number of unstable nuclei – lots of radiation emitted

fewer unstable nuclei – less radiation emitted

half-life

half-life

after each half-life the number of undecayed nuclei halves

after each half-life the activity of the source halves

Half-life graphs

Although half-lives can vary enormously, a graph plotting the **number of undecayed atoms** in a sample **against time** will always have the **same shape**.

A graph plotting the number of undecayed atoms against time has the **same shape** for all radioactive nuclei. A graph plotting count rate against time also has the same shape for all radioactive nuclei.

We can use these graphs to determine the half-lives of radioactive nuclei.

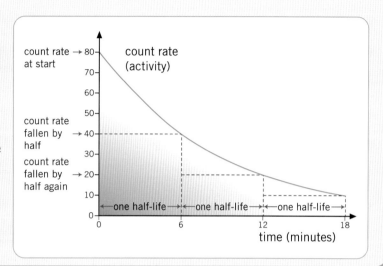

Half-life calculations

Once we know the half-life of a radioactive material we can calculate the number of undecayed nuclei in a sample or its activity after a certain number of half-lives.

Example

The initial activity of a radioisotope is 960 counts per minute.

If the half-life of the radioisotope is 20 minutes, calculate the activity of the source after a) one hour and b) one hour and forty minutes.

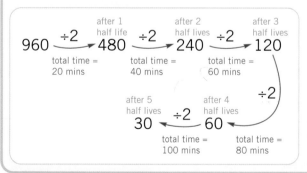

Example

A radioisotope initially contains 8×10^8 undecayed nuclei. After six days, it contains 1×10^8 undecayed nuclei. Calculate the half-life of the isotope.

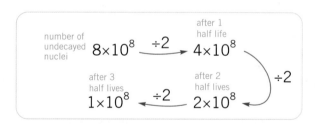

These calculations are very simple. It is, however, easy to make mistakes if you try to do them in your head. To avoid any slips, get into the habit of always writing down the sequence of a decay, as shown in the two examples above.

QUICK TEST

① What is 'radioactive decay'?

② Write a decay equation which describes the following.
 a) Einsteinium (Es) proton number 99 and mass number 253 decays to form Berkelium (Bk) proton number 97 and mass number 249.

 b) Iodine (I) proton number 53 and mass number 128 decays to form Xenon (Xe) proton number 54 and mass number 128.

③ The activity of a radioisotope drops from 600 emissions per minute to 150 emissions per minute in six days. Calculate its half-life.

Uses of radioactivity

Radioactive tracers

Radioisotopes are often used in industry to monitor the flow of **liquids and gases in pipes**.

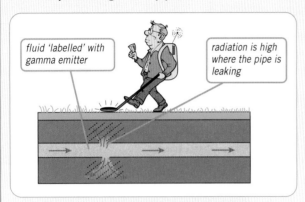

fluid 'labelled' with gamma emitter

radiation is high where the pipe is leaking

If the pipe is underground, a gamma-emitting radioisotope is added to the fluid flowing through it. Gamma-emitting fluid is used as the radiation can be detected at the surface. This material is called a **tracer**. The progress of the tracer through the pipe is tracked using a **detector**. If there is **a leak** in the pipe, **a higher concentration** of gamma radiation will be detected at the point of the leak. If there is a blockage, there will be little or no evidence of radioactivity in the pipe after this point. Using a radioisotope in this manner **avoids the need to dig up whole sections** of roads and piping in order to locate a leak.

Tracers can also be used to check the progress of fluids, such as blood and digested food, through the body. For example, sodium-24 is a radioisotope that can be introduced into the body to check for **internal bleeding**. It has a short half-life and so the body tissue is not exposed to radiation for a long period of time.

Radiotherapy

Some forms of cancer can be removed by surgery. Others, like brain tumours, may require a different solution because of their position, for example that of **radiotherapy**.

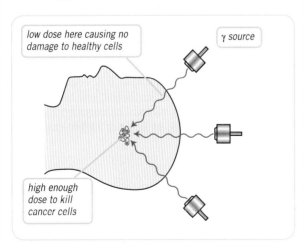

low dose here causing no damage to healthy cells

γ source

high enough dose to kill cancer cells

A beam of radiation is directed at the **tumour** from different positions. The **high dose of radiation** that is needed to kill the cancerous cells only occurs within the tumour. In other places, the dose is not sufficient to cause cell damage.

Carbon dating

Carbon has two isotopes: carbon-12, which is not radioactive, and carbon-14, which is radioactive. While a plant or animal is alive, the ratio of these two isotopes within the organism remains the same. When the organism dies, however, this ratio starts to fall. By measuring the ratio, scientists can determine how long ago the plant or animal died.

For example, carbon-14 has a half-life of 5500 years. If the ratio of carbon-14 to carbon-12 is half the value of that found in living organisms, the plant or animal must have been dead for 5500 years.

Uranium isotopes decay to form isotopes of lead. The age of a sample of rock can be determined by measuring the ratio of uranium and lead isotopes.

This shroud was thought to have been wrapped around the body of Christ until carbon-dating showed it to be just under a thousand years old

Sterilisation

Food rots because of the presence and growth of bacteria. Cooling and freezing slows down the growth of the bacteria but does not prevent it. If food is exposed to gamma radiation before being frozen, the bacteria will be killed and the food will keep for much longer. This process is called **sterilisation**.

Surgical instruments used to be sterilised by putting them in boiling water. Nowadays, these instruments are sterilised by exposing them to gamma radiation.

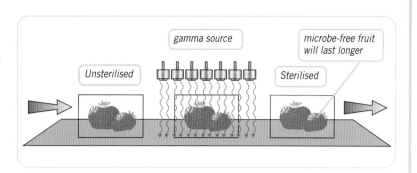

gamma source

microbe-free fruit will last longer

Unsterilised

Sterilised

N.B. germ-free surgical instruments remain germ free until the sealed container is opened

Smoke detectors

Some **smoke detectors**, like the one shown here, contain a small amount of americium-241, which is an **alpha emitter**. The alpha particles emitted by the americium-241 collide with air molecules within the smoke detector, **creating charged particles called ions**. The ions produce a **very small current**. If smoke enters the detector, this **current stops or decreases**. It is this decrease in current that **triggers the alarm**.

One big advantage of using this type of smoke detector is that when its battery is nearing the end of its life, this loss of power will also cause the current to fall and the alarm to sound, so indicating that the battery needs replacing.

The uses of nuclear radiation are a very popular exam topic. Make sure that you can explain some of these uses.

QUICK TEST

1. What is the name given to a radioisotope that is injected into a fluid so that its flow can be monitored?

2. How would using a tracer help us find out if a pipe has a blockage?

3. Why must a tracer that is used to check the flow of blood through a body have a short half-life?

4. What is the treatment of cancer with radiation called?

5. Which type of radiation is used to sterilise surgical instruments?

6. What causes a current to flow in a smoke detector?

7. Which isotope of carbon is used for carbon dating?

Nuclear power

Nuclear power stations and submarines use the *energy stored in the nucleus of an atom*. Controlling the reactions that release this energy is not easy. The photograph on the right shows what can happen if the energy locked inside the nucleus of an atom is released too quickly.

Nuclear fission – splitting the atom

Most atoms with unstable nuclei become more stable by emitting alpha, beta or gamma radiation. Under certain conditions, some nuclei are so unstable that they undergo **nuclear fission**.

Nuclear fission is the splitting of a heavy nucleus into two lighter, more stable nuclei of roughly equal size.

$$^{235}_{92}U + ^{0}_{1}n \xrightarrow{\text{fission reaction}} X + Y + \text{2 or 3 neutrons} + \text{Energy}$$

2 lighter nuclei of roughly equal size

Uranium-235 is an isotope of uranium that can be made to undergo fission. A beam of neutrons is directed at the uranium nucleus. If a neutron is **absorbed by the nucleus**, it may split in two and, at the same time, release several fast-moving neutrons. As a nucleus splits, energy is released.

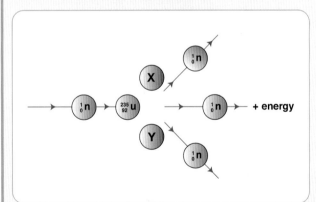

Neutrons ejected by the uranium as it splits may strike other uranium nuclei, releasing even more neutrons and energy. This is an **uncontrolled, accelerating chain reaction**. If unchecked, the release of energy will be so rapid it may cause a **nuclear explosion**.

In order to control the reaction, some of the ejected neutrons must be removed. If **too few** neutrons are removed, the reaction will **continue to accelerate**: if **too many** are removed the reaction will **slow down and stop**. If the **correct number** of neutrons is removed, the

reaction will **neither accelerate nor decelerate**, and the **release of energy will be steady**. This is the basis of a **nuclear reactor**.

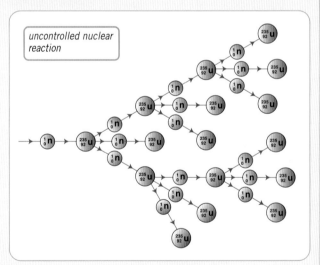

uncontrolled nuclear reaction

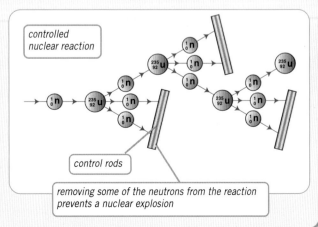

controlled nuclear reaction

control rods

removing some of the neutrons from the reaction prevents a nuclear explosion

The nuclear reactor

Two fissionable substances are commonly used in nuclear reactors: uranium-235 and plutonium-239. The uranium-235 or plutonium-239 is contained in **fuel rods** within the nuclear reactor. Between these fuel rods are **control rods**, made from boron or cadmium. These fuel rods absorb some of the ejected neutrons. By pushing the rods further into the reactor, more neutrons are absorbed and the reaction slows down. Pulling the rods out a little increases the rate of the reaction.

Neutrons ejected from the uranium or plutonium nuclei have speeds that may be too high for them to be absorbed by other nuclei. To improve the chance of interaction a material called a **moderator**, which slows the neutrons down, is placed around the control rods. This is often graphite or 'heavy water'.

In a **pressurised, water-cooled reactor**, water is pumped under pressure through the reactor vessel. The water absorbs energy released by the fission reactions and becomes very hot. This hot water is pumped into a **heat exchanger**, where the steam produced is used to generate electricity.

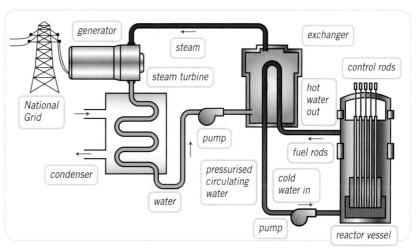

Fusion

Nuclear fusion is the opposite of nuclear fission. Nuclear fusion reactions **join together small nuclei** to make **heavier, more stable nuclei**.

The energy we receive from the Sun is released during fusion reactions when the nuclei of isotopes of **hydrogen and/or helium** join together to produce heavier, more stable nuclei. As the nuclei **join together**, there is a **release of energy**.

Fusion reactions like this are much **cleaner** than fission reactions and produce very little radioactive waste. They are an attractive possibility for producing energy in the future. Unfortunately, we are unable at present to produce the conditions necessary (a temperature of 100 million degrees Centigrade) to start the fusion reaction.

💡 *Don't get these two different types of nuclear reaction mixed up. Remember, fusion glues nuclei together.*

Nuclear fusion reactions like this occur within all stars. It is the process by which energy is released

$$^2_1\text{H} + {}^2_1\text{H} \longrightarrow {}^3_2\text{H} + {}^1_0\text{n} + \text{Energy}$$

light nuclei   *light nuclei*   *heavier more stable nuclei*

QUICK TEST

1. What happens to a nucleus when it undergoes fission?
2. What happens to a nucleus when it undergoes fusion?
3. What is an 'uncontrolled nuclear reaction'?
4. What is a 'controlled nuclear reaction'?
5. Name one substance from which control rods in a nuclear reactor are made.
6. How is the energy produced in a nuclear reactor removed?
7. Give one advantage of using nuclear fusion reactions to supply our energy needs.
8. Where are fusion reactions taking place at present?
9. Why are there no fusion power stations?

Practice questions

Use the questions to test your progress. Check your answers on page 126.

1. Calculate the speed of a runner who travels 200 m in 20 s.

   ....

2. Calculate the distance travelled by a motorist who travels at an average speed of 80 km/h for 5 hours.

   ....

3. Explain how a driver's tiredness can affect the total stopping distance of a vehicle.

   ....

4. The graph below shows the journey of a cyclist.

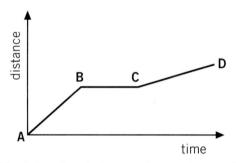

   Explain what is happening to the cyclist between:
   a) A and B ....
   b) B and C ....
   c) C and D ....

5. Why will a sky diver be travelling at a constant speed several seconds after jumping from an aircraft?

   ....

6. An object of mass 5 kg is lifted from the ground and placed onto a shelf 2 m above the floor by a worker.
   a) What kind of energy does the object gain if it is lifted on to a shelf 2 m above the ground?

   ....

   b) If g = 10 N/kg, calculate i) the weight of the object and ii) the work done in lifting the object onto the shelf.

   ....

   c) If the man takes 4 s to lift the object from the ground onto the shelf, what is his power?

   ....

7. An aircraft travels down a runway for 40 s.
   a) If the aircraft starts from rest and has an average acceleration of 4 m/s^2, calculate the final speed of the aircraft.

   ....

   b) If the aircraft has a mass of 10 000 kg, calculate the propulsive force produced by the engines.

   ....

8. Calculate the kinetic energy and momentum of an object which has a mass of 2 kg and is moving at 20 m/s.

   ....

9. If the object in question 8 is brought to rest in 4 s by a retarding force, a) what is the work done by the force and b) calculate the size of the force.

   ....

10. Calculate the momentum of a bullet that has a mass of 10 g (0.01 kg) and is travelling at a velocity of 400 m/s.

   ....

11. Calculate the force necessary to bring a car of mass 500 kg, travelling at 30 m/s, to rest in 10 s.

   ....

12. What is a 'crumple zone'? How will it protect the passengers if a car is involved in an accident?

   ....

13. What is a 'centripetal force'?

   ....

14. What happens when two similarly charged objects are placed next to each other?

   ....

15. Give two uses for static electricity.

   ....

16. To which part of an electrical appliance should the earth wire be connected?

   ....

17. What is a 'light dependent resistor'? Name one use for a light dependent resistor.

   ....

18. Calculate the power of a hairdryer when connected to a 240 V supply that has a current of 5 A flowing through it.

   ....

19. Calculate the resistance of a piece of wire which allows a current of 0.25 A to flow through it when a p.d. of 6 V is applied across its ends.

   ....

20. Calculate the correct value of the fuse that should be included in a 3-pin plug for a 1000 W 240 V hairdryer.

   ....

21. What kind of nuclear reaction:
    a) causes a large nucleus to split into two smaller nuclei? ....
    b) causes two small nuclei to join together to make larger nuclei?...

22. The equations below describe radioactive decay by the emission of an alpha particle and a beta particle.

    $$^{231}_{91}Pa \rightarrow {}^{4}_{2}He + {}^{y}_{x}Ac$$

    $$^{214}_{82}Pb \rightarrow {}^{0}_{-1}e + {}^{q}_{p}Bi$$

    a) What are the values of x and y? ....
    b) What are the values of p and q?...

Answers

SCIENCE SUCCESS

Answers

Biology
Quick test answers
Page 5 Cells
1. A plant cell has chloroplasts, a cell wall and a vacuole
2. Both have mitochondria, a cell membrane, nucleus, cytoplasm and ribosomes
3. It controls what passes in and out of the cell
4. It gives a plant cell extra strength and support
5. Respiration
6. A cell that has changed its shape to do a particular job
7. Red blood cell

Page 7 Diffusion and osmosis
1. e.g. The diffusion of carbon dioxide into a leaf
2. A membrane that only allows small molecules to pass through it
3. Water
4. They become turgid
5. They become flaccid
6. They have no cell wall
7. The movement of a greater number of particles/more water in one direction than the other
8. Hot, dry and windy conditions

Page 9 Photosynthesis
1. To absorb the sunlight hitting the plant on the surface of the leaf: palisade cells contain the most chlorophyll in order to do this job
2. To make the amino acids that make proteins
3. Its growth will be stunted and it will have yellow older leaves
4. Carbon dioxide, water, chlorophyll and light
5. Oxygen and glucose
6. The amount of light and carbon dioxide, and temperature
7. By burning wood and fermenting some plants into alcohol

Page 11 Plant hormones
1. Auxin
2. Geotropism
3. Phototropism
4. Root tips and shoot tips
5. The opposite side (right)
6. Slow down
7. Speed up
8. Growing cuttings
   Killing weeds
   Seedless fruits
   Early ripening
9. Auxin gathers on the lower half of the shoot and speeds up the growth on this side
10. Auxin gathers on the lower half of the root and slows down growth on this side

Page 13 Pyramids of numbers and biomass
1. Energy is lost along the chain
2. The numbers of organisms involved in a food chain
3. The mass of the organisms
4. The Sun
5. They need to keep warm, which uses energy gained through respiration
6. Respiration, heat, waste, and parts of the body not eaten

Page 15 The carbon cycle
1. Photosynthesis

2. Respiration and burning/combustion
3. Animals, plants and decomposers/microorganisms
4. The breaking down of dead material
5. Decomposers, bacteria and fungi and detritovores
6. Turned into fossil fuels eventually
7. Warmth, moisture and oxygen
8. Turn it into carbohydrates, proteins and fat

Page 17 The nitrogen cycle
1. For making proteins
2. Nitrates
3. It causes nitrogen and oxygen to combine at high temperature, dissolve in rain and form nitrates in the soil
4. In the soil and root nodules of some plants
5. In the soil: they convert ammonia from waste and remains into nitrates
6. Bacteria, present in waterlogged soils, which convert nitrates back into nitrogen
7. Taken up by plants dissolved in water or leaching
8. They contain nitrogen-fixing bacteria in their root nodules that convert nitrogen into nitrates
9. They are broken down by detritivores and decomposers into ammonia compounds
10. By eating plants (or animals)

Page 19 Enzymes and digestion
1. In the salivary glands
2. Neutralises stomach acid and emulsifies fat
3. In the small intestine
4. Fatty acids and glycerol
5. Chains of amino acids
6. pH and temperature
7. To pre-digest baby foods

Page 21 Respiration and exercise
1. The breaking down of glucose using oxygen
2. Water and carbon dioxide
3. In the mitochondria of a cell's cytoplasm
4. The time it takes for the heart/pulse rate to return to normal after exercise
5. They are more accurate, remove human error and monitor continuously
6. Liver and kidneys
7. To get oxygen to the muscles
8. To pump the blood delivering oxygen and glucose to the muscles and to remove carbon dioxide more quickly

Page 23 Blood and blood vessels
1. Right
2. Pulmonary vein and vena cava
3. Pulmonary artery and aorta
4. They prevent the blood flowing back into the heart
5. Haemoglobin
6. To withstand the high pressure
7. Veins
8. Capillaries

Page 25 Manipulating life
1. A technique for correcting defective genes responsible for disease
2. Genetically modified

3. The first mammal cloned
4. Artificial selection
5. An individual that is genetically identical to the parent
6. Many wild plant varieties could be killed when spraying herbicide-resistant crops with herbicide, reducing the food source for some insects
7. They can be mass produced quickly and cheaply, and they are all genetically identical

Page 27 Mendel and genetics
1. The colour red
2. The weaker characteristic
3. Genes
4. The inheritance of a single characteristic
5. What an organism looks like physically, as a result of the genes they have
6. The organism must have two of the same alleles, that is, it must be homozygous
7. Homozygous
8. A test cross

Page 29 Growth
1. The limit on the number of cell divisions
2. Stem cells and cancer cells
3. Factors that can enhance performance in sport
4. Mitosis and differentiation
5. The ability to re-grow body parts
6. Root and shoot tips

Page 31 Mitosis
1. Two
2. 46
3. Growth and replacement of cells
4. Coiled strands of DNA
5. One
6. No
7. Clones
8. A cell that has yet to specialise
9. In human embryos and bone marrow
10. Four

Page 33 Meiosis and fertilisation
1. 23
2. 46
3. A fertilised egg
4. 50%
5. 50%
6. Male
7. 19
8. Female

Page 35 Genes, chromosomes and DNA
1. In the nucleus, making up the 'arms' of a chromosome
2. Sections of DNA that code for a particular characteristic or protein
3. Polypeptides
4. 3
5. Ribosomes in the cytoplasm
6. mRNA (messenger RNA)
7. On the chromosomes
8. Protein synthesis
9. 46, nucleus
10. Amino acids

Page 37 Homeostasis
1. It takes away heat energy when it evaporates
2. As a result of vasoconstriction, less blood reaches the surface of the skin

3. Making constant adjustments to maintain the body's internal environment at normal levels
4. Insulin and glucagon
5. Liver
6. It converts it to glycogen for storage
7. The pancreas producing insufficient insulin
8. By insulin injections
9. Cleaning the blood and excretion
10. The regulation of the concentration of water in the blood

Page 39 Farming
1. Manure
2. Organic farming produces less food per area of land. It is also more time consuming and labour intensive to develop crops organically
3. The growth of plants without soil
4. They turn nitrogen into nitrates which fertilise the soil
5. The floor traps heat from the sun and heats up the air that continuously rises and falls
6. By pesticides or specific biological controls
7. Wrasse fish
8. They are contained in nets

Page 41 The environment
1. The chopping down of trees to ground level to allow regrowth and a supply of timber
2. Replanting forests when they have been cut down
3. Replace trees and allow forests to develop again once chopped down
4. They use hydrogen sulphide and oxygen to make energy and then convert the energy into food – this process is called chemosynthesis
5. Bacteria
6. Hydrogen sulphide

Biology
Answers to Practice questions
Page 42
1. It is too cold for the decay process to work
2. carbon dioxide + water → oxygen + glucose (using chlorophyll to absorb light)
3. Temperature and the amount of light and carbon dioxide
4. a) cell wall
   b) cell membrane
   c) cytoplasm
   d) vacuole
   e) chloroplast
   f) nucleus
5. a) cell membrane
   b) nucleus
   c) cytoplasm
6. A plant cell has a cell wall, chloroplasts and a permanent vacuole
7. 46
8. In the ovaries and testes, produces sperms and eggs
9. Osmosis
10. 37°C
11. The body doesn't produce enough insulin and the blood sugar level is too high
12. By injections of insulin
13. a) Lowers blood sugar levels
    b) Raises blood sugar levels

124

14. They dilate allowing blood to the surface of the skin
15. Phenotype is the physical appearance and the genotype is the genes an organism possesses
16. 23
17. The liver stores excess glucose as glycogen and converts it back to glucose when needed
18. In the mitochondria of cells
19. The sex cells, sperms and eggs
20. Diploid means it contains 46 chromosomes, body cells contain 46 chromosomes
21. The limit to the number of times a cell can divide in the body
22. Root tips and shoot tips
23. Denitrifying bacteria, nitrifying bacteria and nitrogen-fixing bacteria
24. Warmth, moisture and oxygen
25. DNA replication
26. 46
27. Grow food in greenhouses and fish farms
28. Lack of water causes water to move out of the cells and they become flaccid
29. It shows the numbers of organisms involved in food chains and also the mass of the organisms involved
30. Asexual reproduction involves one parent and offspring are identical, sexual reproduction involves two parents and offspring show variation

Chemistry
Quick test answers
Page 45 Atomic structure
1. Protons and neutrons
2. Electrons
3. Charge +1, mass 1 amu
4. Charge −1, mass negligible
5. No charge, mass 1 amu
6. Number of protons + number of neutrons
7. Number of protons
8. Atomic number/number of protons/number of electrons
9. Mass number/number of neutrons
10. They have the same number of electrons and so the same electron structure

Page 47 Balancing equations
1. Three (calcium, carbon and oxygen)
2. Calcium
3. One carbon and one oxygen atom
4. One carbon and two oxygen atoms
5. One sulphur and two oxygen atoms
6. Atoms cannot be created or destroyed during chemical reactions
7. $2Na + Cl_2 \rightarrow 2NaCl$
8. $H_2 + Cl_2 \rightarrow 2HCl$
9. $C + CO_2 \rightarrow 2CO$
10. It is a liquid

Page 49 Ionic and covalent bonding
1. 1
2. 6
3. 1+
4. 2−
5.
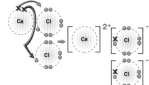

6. Strong attraction between oppositely charged ions
7. Covalent
8.
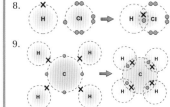
9.

Page 51 Ionic and covalent structures
1. Giant ionic regular
2. Strong forces of attraction between oppositely charged ions
3. When dissolved, the ions can move
4. When molten, the ions can move
5. Water, hydrogen iodide and methane
6. There is a strong attraction between atoms but a weak attraction between molecules
7. No
8. Diamonds and graphite
9. Lots of very strong covalent bonds
10. Bonding between the layers is weak and so these electrons can conduct electricity

Page 53 Group 1 – the alkali metals
1. Lithium, sodium and potassium
2. One
3. They have the same outer electron structure
4. Ionic
5. 1+
6. Increases down the group
7. It is less dense than water
8. It burns with a squeaky pop
9. $2Na + 2H_2O \rightarrow 2NaOH + H_2$
10. $2Na + Cl_2 \rightarrow 2NaCl$

Page 55 Group 7 – the halogens
1. Halogens
2. Increases
3. Decreases
4. Use a fume cupboard, goggles and gloves
5. Increases
6. Gas, gas, liquid, solid
7. Colour gets darker (pale yellow, pale green, brown, dark grey/purple)
8. Water purification and manufacture of pesticides and plastics
9. Antiseptic
10. Displacement reaction gives potassium chloride + bromine

Page 57 Metals
1. They have free/delocalised electrons
2. Middle section
3. High melting point, high density, shiny, tough, hard wearing, form coloured compounds and are good catalysts
4. Good electrical conductor which can be bent
5. Does not corrode or fracture
6. Iron is brittle
7. Bridges, buildings, ships, cars and trains, among many others
8. Haber process
9. Coins
10. Margarine

Page 59 Relative formula mass
1. 23
2. 28
3. 32
4. 40
5. 64

6. 5%
7. 60%
8. 60%
9. 40%
10. 50%

Page 61 Calculating masses
1. hydrogen + oxygen → water
2. $2H_2 + O_2 \rightarrow 2H_2O$
3. 36 g
4. 144 g
5. 90 g
6. magnesium + oxygen → magnesium oxide
7. $2Mg + O_2 \rightarrow 2MgO$
8. 18 g
9. 48 g
10. 63%

Page 63 Reversible reactions
1. It can proceed in either direction
2. Exothermic
3. Endothermic
4. They must be the same
5. Where nothing can enter or leave
6. Where the rate of forward and backward reactions are the same and there is no change in the overall concentrations of reactants or products
7. Decrease the yield
8. Increase the yield
9. Increase the yield
10. Decrease the yield

Page 65 The Haber process
1. Ammonia
2. Natural gas
3. Air
4. The reaction can go forwards or backwards
5. There are fewer gas molecules on the products side of the equation
6. A high pressure increases the yield of ammonia
7. It increases the yield
8. It decreases the rate of reaction
9. It gives a reasonable yield fairly quickly
10. Iron

Page 67 Rates of reaction
1. Activation energy
2. Decreases
3. Increases
4. Increases
5. Increases
6. Increases
7. They are not used up during a reaction
8. By how fast the reactants are used up and product is made
9. By increasing the temperature, increasing the concentration or pressure, increasing the surface area, or adding a catalyst
10. Not necessarily – catalysts are specific to chemical reactions

Page 69 Exothermic and endothermic reactions
1. Exothermic
2. Energy has to be supplied for the reaction to take place
3. It releases lots of energy
4. Exothermic
5. No, energy can be released in other forms such as light, sound or electrical
6. Supplied
7. The amount of energy that must be taken in to break one mole of bonds
8. Released
9. Exothermic, we burn fuels to release energy in the form of heat
10. 2060 kJ mol^{-1}

Page 71 Electrolysis of sodium chloride solution
1. 1 and 7
2. Sea and underground deposits
3. Salt lowers the freezing point of water
4. Sodium chloride dissolved in water
5. Chlorine
6. Hydrogen
7. Sodium hydroxide
8. Bleach, purification of water, production of hydrochloric acid and PVC
9. Manufacture of margarine
10. Soap, detergents, paper, rayon, acetate

Page 73 Acids, bases and neutralisation
1. H^+
2. OH^-
3. Hydrochloric acid, sulphuric acid and nitric acid
4. They are completely ionised
5. Ethanoic acid, citric acid and carbonic acid
6. Ammonia
7. They are not fully ionised
8. The concentration of hydrogen ions
9. Potassium chloride
10. Potassium nitrate

Page 75 Making salts
1. Potassium chloride + water
2. Sodium sulphate + water
3. Carbon dioxide
4. Zinc chloride + water + carbon dioxide
5. Magnesium sulphate + water + carbon dioxide
6. Remove any unreacted solid by filtering, and then evaporate the water
7. Magnesium chloride + hydrogen
8. Zinc sulphate + hydrogen
9. Zinc chloride + water
10. Copper sulphate + water

Page 77 Chemical tests
1. When bubbled through limewater it turns the limewater cloudy
2. The gas bleaches damp litmus paper
3. Relights a glowing splint
4. It burns with a squeaky pop
5. Carbon dioxide
6. Green
7. Lilac
8. Orange
9. Green
10. Pale blue

Page 79 Water
1. Filtering
2. Chlorine is added
3. Eutrophication
4. Nitrates, lead compounds and pesticides

Page 81 Uses of oils and alcohol
1. Fruits, seeds or nuts
2. Seeds
3. A and D
4. Fats have higher boiling points
5. Fried foods have more energy
6. Saturated
7. Lots of double bonds
8. Easier to spread, can be used to make cakes and pastries, and have a longer shelf life
9. Nickel
10. Phosphoric acid

Chemistry
Answers to Practice questions
Page 82
1. a) zinc sulphate
   b) sodium nitrate
   c) insoluble barium sulphate

    d) copper chloride
2. a) So that the ions can move
  b) $Pb^{2+} + 2e^- \rightarrow Pb$
  c) $2Cl^- - 2e^- \rightarrow Cl_2$
3. a) diamond
  b) A
  c) D
  d) D
  e) A
  f) B and C
  g) NO
4. a) electron
  b) A
  c) A
  d) C
  e) 1 amu
  f) B and C
  g) B and C
  h) A and C
5. a) $2H^+ + 2e^- \rightarrow H_2$
  b) $2Cl^- - 2e^- \rightarrow Cl_2$
  c) Sterilising water, bleaching, the manufacture of hydrochloric acid and the manufacture of PVC [any one of these]
6. a) Use a fume cupboard, wear goggles and gloves
  b) chlorine + potassium bromide → bromine + potassium chloride
  c) $Cl_2 + 2KBr \rightarrow Br_2 + 2KCl$
7. a) D
  b) B
  c) B
  d) C
  e) A
  f) B
  g) D
  h) A
  i) C
  j) A
8. a) 36.4%
  b) The reaction is reversible and does not go to completion; some of the product is lost during filtering or evaporation, when transferring liquids or during heating; there may be side-reactions occurring that produce other products

Physics
Quick test answers
Page 85 Speed, velocity and acceleration
1. 5 m/s
2. 55 s
3. Speed tells us how fast an object is moving, e.g. 5 m/s. Velocity tells us the speed of an object and its direction, e.g. 5 m/s westwards
4. 3 m/s^2
5. 50 m/s
6. 8 s

Page 87 Graphs of motion
1. a) a stationary object
  b) greater constant speed
  c) lesser constant speed
2. a) constant speed
  b) large acceleration
  c) small deceleration

Page 89 Balanced and unbalanced forces
1. No effect
2. They cause a change of direction or speed
3. The mass of an object and the size of the force
4. 20 N

Page 91 Frictional forces and terminal velocity
1. The force that opposes motion
2. The opposite direction to motion
3. a) travels at a constant velocity
  b) slows down
4. Making himself into a streamlined shape
5. 650 N

Page 93 Stopping distance
1. The distance a vehicle travels before the brakes are applied
2. The distance the vehicle travels whilst the brakes are being applied
3. The total distance the driver needs to bring a vehicle to a halt
4. Frictional forces
5. a) The older the driver the slower his reactions and so the greater the thinking distance
  b) If a driver has been travelling for a long time and is tired, his reactions will be slower and the thinking distance greater as a result
  c) The driver will have faster reactions and so the thinking distance will be shorter
6. a) The larger the mass, the greater the braking distance
  b) The greater the speed, the larger the braking distance
  c) The smoother the tyres and the road surface, the smaller the frictional forces and so the larger the braking distance
7. a) 18 m
  b) 60 m
  c) 78 m (approx. values)

Page 95 Work and power
1. 7500 J
2. 40 m
3. 1500 N
4. Rate of doing work
5. a) joules
  b) watts
6. 300 W
7. 500 W

Page 97 Kinetic energy and potential energy
1. a) The energy an object possesses because of its movement
  b) The energy an object possesses because of its position in a gravitational field
2. 90 J
3. 300 J

Page 99 Momentum
1. Momentum is a measure of how difficult it is to alter how an object is moving
2. 9000 kg m/s
3. 2000 N
4. The crumple zones increase the time that cars take to slow down during collisions and so reduce the forces on the driver and passengers. Without crumple zones, the forces would be much stronger and more dangerous
5. They increase the time of momentum change and so the size of the decelerating forces

Page 101 Collisions and explosions
1. When two or more bodies act on each other, their total momentum remains constant, providing there is no external force acting
2. 5 m/s
3. 5 m/s
4. 5 m/s

Page 103 Motion in a circle
1. It moves in a constant direction at a constant speed
2. Zero resultant force
3. It is continually changing direction
4. It always acts towards the centre of the circle: it becomes bigger

Page 105 Static electricity
1. Protons and electrons
2. There are equal numbers of each
3. Electrons
4. Conductors allow charges to flow through them: insulators do not
5. Paint spraying, photocopying, removing dust from smoke [any of these or similar]
6. Danger of sparks and explosions

Page 107 Circuits, currents and resistance
1. A flow of charge
2. a) electrons
  b) ions
3. Several cells connected together
4. Complete
5. a) series
  b) parallel
6. ohms (Ω)
7. To control streetlighting
8. 4.5 Ω

Page 109 Domestic electricity
1. AC
2. a) brown
  b) green and yellow
  c) blue
3. This metal is a very good conductor
4. It can be reset
5. When using an electric lawn mower or hedge trimmers

Page 111 Electrical power
1. a) 6000 J
  b) 30 kJ
  c) 36 kJ
  d) 60 kJ
  e) 120 kJ
2. 20 W
3. 690 W
4. 3 A

Page 113 The structure of atoms
1. Nuclear atom
2. Nucleus
3. −1
4. Same number
5. 8, 14

Page 115 Nuclear radiations
1. Damage cells, kills cells, cancer
2. They are unstable
3. In order for us to choose the most appropriate
4. a) Gamma
  b) Alpha
  c) Beta
  d) Beta
  e) Gamma

Page 117 Radioactive decay
1. The emission of alpha, beta or gamma radiation from a nucleus
2. a) $^{253}_{99}Es \rightarrow ^{249}_{97}Bk + ^4_2He$
  b) $^{128}_{53}I \rightarrow ^{128}_{54}Xe + ^0_{-1}e$
3. Three days

Page 119 Uses of radioactivity
1. A tracer
2. No radioactivity would be detected after the blockage
3. To minimise any cell damage that might be caused by the radiation
4. Radiotherapy
5. Gamma
6. The creation of ions by the alpha emitter
7. Carbon-14

Page 121 Nuclear power
1. It splits
2. It joins with another nucleus
3. Energy released too quickly
4. Energy released at a steady rate
5. Boron or cadmium
6. Using pressurised water
7. It is cleaner and produces no radioactive waste
8. In the Sun and stars
9. The starting temperature for the reaction is too high

Physics
Answers to Practice questions
Page 122
1. 10 m/s
2. 400 km
3. If a driver is tired, his reactions will be slower than normal and, therefore, his thinking distance and overall stopping distance will increase
4. a) The cyclist is travelling at a constant speed
  b) The cyclist has stopped
  c) The cyclist is moving at a constant speed but slower than between A and B
5. Air resistance and gravitational forces will be equal and balanced
6. a) gravitational potential energy
  b) 50 N, 100 J
  c) 25 W
7. a) 160 m/s
  b) 40 000 N
8. 400 J and 40 kg m/s
9. a) 400 J (same as its KE)
  b) 10 N
10. 4 kg m/s
11. 1500 N
12. Part of a car that is designed to crumple and absorb some of the energy of the collision during an accident so that the deceleration experienced by the passengers is lessened
13. The forces that causes objects to move in a circle
14. They repel
15. Electrostatic spraying and precipitation, photocopying [any two, or similar]
16. The outer casing
17. A resistor whose resistance is greatly altered by changes in light intensity: an automatic lighting control
18. 1200 W
19. 24 Ω
20. 5 A
21. a) fission
  b) fusion
22. a) 89 and 227
  b) 83 and 214